STRATEGIC DISAGREEMENT

Stalemate in American Politics

JOHN B. GILMOUR

UNIVERSITY OF PITTSBURGH PRESS

Pittsburgh and London

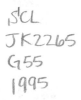

For Ann, who is most agreeable

Published by the University of Pittsburgh Press, Pittsburgh, Pa., 15260
Copyright © 1995, University of Pittsburgh Press
All rights reserved
Manufactured in the United States of America
Printed on acid-free paper

Library of Congress Cataloging-in-Publication Data

Gilmour, John B.
    Strategic disagreement : stalemate in American politics / John B.
Gilmour.
        p.   cm. — (Pitt series in policy and institutional studies)
    ISBN 0-8229-3907-X (cloth : acid-free paper). —ISBN
0-8229-5575-X (pbk. : acid-free paper)
    1. Political parties—United States.   2. Politics, Practical—
United States.   3. United States—Politics and government—1993–
I. Title. II. Series.
JK2265.G55   1995
324'.0973—dc20   95-32777
                                                             CIP

A CIP catalogue record for this book is available from the British Library.
Eurospan, London

Contents

Acknowledgments

Just because a book is short does not mean the author has not received a great deal of help. Morris Fiorina and David Mayhew both read a complete draft and provided exceptionally useful advice. Bert Rockman was a most encouraging series editor. Joe White, Steve Weatherford, John Huber, George Tsebelis, Bill Lowry, Steve Stedman, Jack Knight, Bill Caspary, John Sprague, Nelson Polsby, and Mike McKuen helped by reading the manuscript, or portions thereof, and talking with me about it. A conversation with Nick Masters started me on the line of thinking that led to this book. Robert J. Myers saved me from many errors of fact in chapter 5 concerning the Social Security program. Mike Rothberg, Kevin Corder, Paul Gerew, Russ Adams, Mike Johnson, and Faysal El-Hasham were all useful research assistants. Larry Grossback, Nicole Collins, and Andy Whitford, graduate students at Washington University, read the manuscript and provided useful suggestions and comments. Jim Layerzapf of the Eisenhower Library in Abilene, Kansas, helped me find documents both when I was in Abilene and later when I called for more help. The Brookings Institution provided a stimulating environment and a place to hook up my computer while I spent a summer in Washington.

I am grateful to them all.

STRATEGIC DISAGREEMENT

Stalemate in American Politics

Introduction: Strategies of Disagreement

There's nothing in the middle of the road
but yellow stripes and dead armadillos.
—*Jim Hightower*

Passing important national legislation in the United States almost always requires contending parties and factions to accept compromises that give them less than they really want. The hundred days under Franklin D. Roosevelt stands out as an exception, but normally no party or faction has sufficient dominance over Congress and the presidency to enact unilateral solutions, and thus they must bargain with contending interests to assemble a broad supporting coalition.[1] One might think that politicians would accept as inevitable compromises that help a bill to pass—even when they are distasteful and water down a proposal—provided the resulting legislation improves on existing policy from their point of view. Yet politicians frequently reject compromise because the political advantages of maintaining disagreements outweigh the benefits of a modestly better policy achieved through compromise.

Political negotiations can be extremely difficult to conclude successfully because politicians need to maintain and satisfy the coalition that elected them, yet the actions calculated to generate constituency loyalty tend to undermine negotiations. The converse is true as well. A willingness to compromise, essential to reaching an agreement, does not inspire the loyalty of constituents and can erode support for the politicians who negotiate compromises.[2]

This is a book about strategies of disagreement, the efforts of politicians to avoid reaching an agreement when compromise might alienate supporters, damage their prospects in an upcoming election, or preclude getting a better deal in the future. The phenomenon is not extremely common but has important consequences because the issues affected are among the most conspicuous, including health care, education, welfare, and the budget deficit. Strategies of disagreement can delay the enactment of significant legislation, to the detriment of the intended beneficiaries, and can lead to a perception of paralysis when the government does not respond to perceived problems.

Politicians may prefer disagreement to compromise for several reasons. Explaining the necessity of compromise to enthusiastic followers can be difficult, and consequently, leaders who initiate and support compromise sometimes find themselves reviled as traitors rather than praised as pragmatic leaders. Politicians also like to maintain their distinctiveness from their competitors on issues where they believe they have an advantage. Agreeing to a compromise reduces their distinctiveness and diminishes their advantage over rivals.[3] Moreover, there are times when accepting half a loaf can make it difficult or impossible to get the whole loaf later on; therefore, politicians will avoid compromise when they believe they will be able to get all they want later.

Strategic disagreement takes a variety of forms. In the most common, a party that has an advantage in an issue refuses overtures from the other side, even when the compromise offered improves on the existing policy. If the contending parties are persistent in efforts to outdo each other, a bidding war can result. Under divided party government, the party controlling Congress can underscore the differences between the parties by provoking a veto, that is, by passing a bill they know the president will have to veto. In another scenario, when a serious problem demands attention and requires expensive solutions, contending parties and factions may refuse to engage in serious negotiations and instead issue self-serving proposals that informed people know cannot possibly be adopted. Their actions further a stalemate that will produce a catastrophic outcome, far worse than an unpleasant compromise.

A preference for disagreement over compromise can result occasionally in crazy bidding wars that produce unfortunate legislation, but more often it prevents bills from passing. By adding yet another obstruction to the enactment of legislation, enhancing an already impressive list provided courtesy of the Constitution, strategies of disagreement contribute to a traditional disorder in American national government—a susceptibility to stalemate, deadlock, and (in the current terminology) gridlock.[4] These diagnoses are normally prompted by a lack of legislative response to significant problems, or by the appearance of unseemly conflict in government. It is important to note that strategies of disagreement are but one, albeit important, cause of government inaction, analytically distinct from other causes.

The underlying cause of deadlock is a fragmented political structure in which factions are able to block legislation and which consequently requires broad agreement for legislation to pass. Important legislation generally passes by overwhelming margins because it is only through the accommodation of divergent views that legislation of widespread impact can pass.[5] Whether you approve or disapprove of this feature of American politics depends primarily on whose ox is being gored at the moment. Liberals complained in the late 1950s and early 1960s, when the liberal agenda was being blocked, but after Ronald Reagan's election as president in 1980, liberals were pleased to avail themselves occasionally of obstructionist tactics in order to stand up to a conservative onslaught.[6] The government structure explains why stalemates easily result, but not why particular cases result in stalemates. To understand that, we must look more carefully at the preferences of the members of Congress, and the manner in which they bargain.

In examining stalemate and deadlock, we can distinguish between two important categories—those in which there is no zone of agreement among the parties whose consent is needed, and those where a zone of agreement exists. Let us say that, to deal with a certain problem, there is one set of policies that Democrats are willing to adopt, and another that Republicans would support, and that the assent of both is needed to pass a bill. The overlap or intersection between these two sets is the "zone of agreement," the set of all possible proposals that could be adopted. Where there is no zone of agreement, failure to reach an agreement reflects the preferences of the parties and the constraints imposed by the political system. Where there is a zone of agreement, failure to reach an agreement reflects problems of bargaining.[7]

No zone of agreement exists when prominent policy proposals are extremely far apart. For most of the 1950s, the dominant liberal wing of the Democratic party endorsed some form of health insurance for the aged. President Eisenhower, leader of the Republicans, insisted that no problem existed for which a government solution was required. In this case, no zone of agreement existed because Republicans were satisfied with the status quo and saw no reason to change.

A zone of agreement exists when there is a possible policy change that would bring the existing policy closer to the prominent policy proposals of both major parties or contending factions. In 1960, when the Eisenhower administration endorsed an ambitious health care plan, though one not identical to the Democratic plan, there was a zone of agreement. Since the existing policy was no program at all, to the Democrats even the imperfect Republican plan represented a vast improvement over the status quo.

Apart from the difficulties imposed by the Constitution, the most durable impediment to a negotiated settlement of important public

problems is simple disagreement on what to do—the absence of any
zone of agreement. When no one faction or party can impose its
preferred solution, it must negotiate with rivals to produce a proposal that is satisfactory to everyone with the power to block it. It
may be that while one side sees a terrible problem, the other finds
existing policy entirely satisfactory. This was the case concerning
health care for the elderly throughout much of the 1950s. Liberal
Democrats saw a crisis in health care for the aged, but Representative
Charles Halleck of Indiana, a leading conservative voice, denied there
was a problem with his characteristic sensitivity and understanding:
"If people were dying left and right for lack of medical care, you'd
read about it in the papers."[8] With a fundamental disagreement
about what should be done, or even whether anything should be
done, action is unlikely. Over time, as an idea "germinates," a greater
measure of agreement is likely to develop and the conditions for a
negotiated solution improve.[9]

If both sides recognize there is a problem, disagreement about the
means of solving it can make legislation impossible. In a common
scenario, liberal Democrats propose a regulatory scheme to deal with
a problem. Republicans may be so horrified by interference with
market incentives, or by costs imposed on business or government,
that they cannot go along with the Democratic plan. Or it may be
that while both sides agree there is a problem, they so sharply disagree about its severity and the cost of inaction that no agreement is
possible.

When the cause of government inactivity is real disagreement between competing factions, the problem is not of bargaining or negotiations, but rather of too much conflict in the government, or of a
government structure that penalizes slim majorities. In these cases
there are a number of solutions of varying feasibility, among them:
holding a new election in hopes of producing a decisive majority,
amending the Constitution to limit the ability of minorities to ob-
struct, reducing social conflict, or generating broader areas of agree-

ment. Probably the best way to forge an agreement is to make a problem worse or more obvious, or to increase public awareness of it, which tends to increase the cost of not acting and to make solutions that are less than perfect seem preferable to inaction.[10]

An aspect of political bargaining that often discourages agreement, or at least minimizes pressure on negotiators to reach a settlement, is the absence of a deadline for an agreement on most issues. Without a consensus, a decision can normally be delayed indefinitely until an agreement emerges. This is good in that it allows contentious issues to be deferred, reducing the level of conflict in government; but without pressure on them, negotiators may become unwilling to accept compromises and may hold out for the perfect deal.[11]

There are also cases where a zone of agreement exists but the contending parties never reach it. This is a bargaining failure. Bargaining failure occurs when Congress and the president do not reach agreement on measures that, considered from the standpoint of the disagreeing parties, represent an improvement over existing policy. Such bargaining failures are serious matters, for they represent lost opportunities that may not be redeemed for years. Constituents are deprived of the benefits of legislation.

Bargaining failures come in two varieties. The first is when incompetence, poor communication, or other misadventure prevent negotiators who are otherwise so inclined from reaching an accommodation. Tactics can go awry, with one party employing a hard-nosed style that so puts off the other side that negotiations break off and never resume. The solution is better bargaining and the study of books such as *The Art and Science of Negotiation*, the writing of which was stimulated by the author's view that there is a great deal of inept bargaining.[12]

A second kind of bargaining failure occurs when there is a zone of agreement, but at least one side deliberately avoids it. Here we enter the realm of strategic disagreement. The very existence of these strategies is problematic and puzzling. In some cases it may involve a betrayal of the fiduciary responsibility of representatives to their constituents. The bargaining failures that result, while possibly beneficial to the elected officials who cause them, come at the expense of the intended beneficiaries of laws that do not pass. Democrats, who avoided compromise with Republicans over Medicare legislation in 1960, were not able to pass their preferred form of the law until 1965.[13] Liberals refused to support Nixon's welfare reform proposal in 1969, deeming it pathetically inadequate despite its increase of billions of dollars in spending on the poor. That opportunity has passed forever, for neither Nixon nor any of his successors has been able to pass a similar bill, and the prospect that such a bill will pass in the future now appears close to nil.[14]

The strategies discussed in this book are quite diverse, ranging from stalemates to bidding wars. Their underlying unity lies in the fact that all strategies follow from the efforts of one group, or possibly two, to avoid the best agreement that can be gotten under the circumstances in order to seek political gain. Pursuit and avoidance strategies occur when one group or party tries to take away or diminish the advantage enjoyed by its opponent in a policy area. Rather than take advantage of the new flexibility of its formerly recalcitrant opponent to pass a bill, the threatened party holds itself aloof and refuses compromises, or even increases its bid in order to avoid an agreement that would improve on the status quo. In another set of cases agreement between the two sides is needed to avoid an unthinkable disaster, and for both sides a compromise involving mutual concessions is better than disaster. Yet stalemate results because neither side wishes to make the necessary concessions, and so the problem, for which the solution is obvious, goes unresolved. By contrast, strategic encroachment is not a bargaining failure; the behavior of one side only makes it appear that there is a zone of agreement when in fact there is none. Strategic encroachment may occur when one side expects that the other will strategically disagree. This side tries to gain favor with constituencies by offering a legislative proposal it does not want passed, hoping the other side will not allow it to pass.

Chapter 1, "A Bill or an Issue?" identifies reasons why politicians, under certain conditions, prefer disagreement to compromise. First, political parties and politicians want to be distinct from their competitors, especially on issues where they have an advantage (as the Democrats currently have in the health care area). This is akin to product differentiation in marketing. If a party accepts a compromise, it ceases to be clearly distinguishable from its competitor and loses a valuable advantage, including the ability to attack and criticize the opposition. Second, even though compromise may be absolutely essential to reach an agreement, and an agreement will make followers better off, politicians often find it difficult to explain to supporters why compromise was needed. Compromise can easily be interpreted by enthusiastic supporters of an idea as a sellout or weakness. Competing politicians can accuse those who commit the crime of compromise of betrayal and try to steal their supporters. Third, accepting half a loaf today may preclude getting the whole thing at a later date. Piecemeal reform can, by alleviating the worst consequences of a problem, undermine the support needed to implement more sweeping changes later. Thus, supporters of comprehensive reform often oppose meliorative measures.

The rest of the book is an application of this perspective, an explanation of the kinds of political bargaining produced by a disinclination to compromise, with special attention to the differences between divided and unified party government. Two chapters ("Strategies of Pursuit and Avoidance" and "The Strategy of Encroachment") deal with situations in which one party is perceived to have an advantage with a given constituency group, and the other would like to minimize or erase that advantage. Each chapter characterizes a situation and the pattern of bargaining associated with it, and analyzes several important cases in depth.

"Strategies of Pursuit and Avoidance" analyzes patterns of bidding and bargaining when politicians of varying ideologies compete for the favor of a single, popular constituency—such as the elderly. A party that seeks to overcome a political disadvantage pursues its opponent by making a proposal that puts them relatively close together, a form of "strategic agreement." Then, rather than lose an advantage, the other party avoids an agreement by one of several means. Typically, Republicans and conservative Democrats are disadvantaged in their efforts to win the loyalty of elderly voters because they cannot propose spending increases as readily as liberal Democrats. Democrats seeking the presidential nomination of their party may compete among themselves to see who can offer the most to the elderly. In competition between the parties, Republicans can try to outbid the Democrats in an effort to show that Republicans are as reliable in their support as Democrats. Unwilling to sacrifice their leadership, the Democrats often bid up the Republican offer still further. I consider pursuit and avoidance in general terms and examine it in specific situations, including: a bidding war over Social Security benefits in 1972; strategic avoidance of an agreement on Medicare legislation by Democrats in 1960, which helped delay the adoption of Medicare until 1965; and Senator Edward Kennedy's efforts to avoid an agreement on health care legislation with President Jimmy Carter, as part of his effort to win the Democratic nomination in 1980.

When the supporters of federal action to deal with a problem begin to win favor with a valued constituency, the opponents can work to offset that advantage by means of "strategic encroachment," discussed in chapter 3. Even politicians who want no bill at all recognize that it may become dangerous to be seen wholly in opposition, and unwise to allow supporters of action to have an issue all to themselves. In this devious ploy, the stand-patters make a proposal that positions them close to, but short of, the activists. Many of the ostensible supporters of this proposal do not want to see it adopted, and they count on stubborn activists to reject compromise and keep a bill from being passed. Taking a position allows them to limit their political damage on the issue and keep their opponents from getting all the credit. When the activists do not accept the compromise proposal, stand-patters can say it was activist unreasonableness that killed the bill. It can be awkward for the stand-patters should the activists unexpectedly agree to the proposal, for then those who really prefer to do nothing will be forced to fight their own bill. This has happened on several occasions, most prominently in 1957 when the Democrats unexpectedly accepted a Republican substitute amendment to a school construction bill, forcing the Republicans to kill their own amendment.

Chapter 4, "Provoking a Veto" examines efforts of one party to increase or enhance its advantage in an issue area by passing a bill that a president of the other party will be compelled to veto. It has sometimes been a deliberate strategy to provoke a veto in order to show in the clearest possible way the difference between the two parties.

Chapter 5, "Stalemates and Summit Negotiations," considers another class of disagreements that results when Democrats and Republicans find themselves appealing to different constituencies in a policy dispute. In budgetary disputes, for example, the Republicans may assert their credentials as a party of low taxes while the Democrats strive to show themselves as the leading protectors of Social Security and other programs. In seeking to ingratiate themselves with these different constituencies, the parties will tend to adopt extreme positions and, rather than move closer together, may actually move further apart over the course of negotiations. This produces an extremely durable stalemate. In certain cases, where the failure to act will bring about horrific consequences, a compromise that hurts both sides similarly is better for both sides than not acting and allowing catastrophe to occur. But both sides may prefer disagreement to a compromise that will hurt their standing with constituents. Summit negotiations conducted in private can be very useful in overcoming such stalemates, for they allow negotiators to obscure the origin of necessary compromises. In this chapter I treat several cases in detail, among them the Social Security stalemate and summit of 1981–1983, and the budget impasse of 1987, which was ultimately broken by use of summit negotiations. I conclude that summit negotiations work best when the alternative to an agreement is an inevitable, tremendous disaster that will hurt both sides.

Chapter 6, "Advice to Moral Politicians," concludes the book with a plainly normative argument that politicians should not engage in strategic disagreement when it risks delaying the enactment of legislation that could do some good for constituents. I take particular issue with the notion that enacting a modest program today can prevent the enactment of a better plan later. First, enacting a modest plan may make it easier, not harder, to adopt improvements later, especially if having a program in place helps to mobilize a constituency to lobby for improvements. Second, eschewing a modest plan today in favor of a better one later can be terribly risky, for the opportunity to adopt a better plan may be much further in the future than expected.

1   A Bill or an Issue?

A thing moderately good is not
as good as it ought to be.
—*Thomas Paine*

Common sense and theory both suggest that people should agree to proposals that make them better off. Roy Wilkins, civil rights leader, once explained, "If you are digging a trench with a teaspoon, and a man comes along and offers you a spade, there is something wrong with your head if you turn it down because he didn't offer you a bulldozer."[1] But if we accept this logic, many politicians evidently have something wrong with their heads, because it is entirely possible that Congress will insist on the bulldozer and that no deal will be reached.

Consider the following situation. Congress, controlled by the Democratic party, has long favored legislation to set up a federal health care program estimated to cost some $80 billion each year. The president, a Republican, has expressed firm disapproval, and consequently legislation has made no progress. Now suppose that the president reverses his position and decides to support a similar health care program, but says he will not sign a bill costing more than $40 billion. The Democrats in Congress do not anticipate being able to override a veto. What happens next? Do the Democrats accede to the President's proposal and pass a $40 billion law? Do they first test whether the president is bluffing by passing an $80 billion bill and then, if it is vetoed, pass one the president will sign? Or do they refuse to compromise and hold out for the whole thing?

There are strong reasons for believing that Congress should accept the President's proposal. Congressional Democrats can pass a bill only by obtaining the agreement of the president, and vice versa. Without legislation there is no health program at all and spending is zero, which hurts Democratic constituents more. For the Democrats to spurn a $40 billion offer as a trivial improvement over the status quo seems a reckless abrogation of legislators' responsibility to their constituents.

Now suppose that instead of offering $40 billion, the president meets the Democratic proposal exactly, at $80 billion. What happens then? Again, there are strong reasons for believing that agreement on legislation should be almost immediately forthcoming—after all, when offered exactly what they have requested, most people accept. Yet under similar circumstances Congress has frustrated an agreement by increasing its demand, or used the president's new flexibility to drive a better bargain—say for $100 billion.

Politicians' motivations are complex, for they must satisfy not just themselves but also their constituents. Their seemingly perverse unwillingness to compromise is due to perfectly sensible political calculations. They are interested not only in enacting legislation, but also in retaining their offices, and there are occasions when extremism, stridency, and inflexibility are more expedient than compromise.

One can hardly overestimate the importance of compromise to democratic government. As Mark A. Peterson writes, "If there is one word that epitomizes the workings of government, it is 'compromise'. . . . The idea of accepting less than one wants . . . may be the most universal mechanism of collective decision making in and out of the public sector."[2] Speaker Rayburn's famous advice to new members of the House—"to get along, go along"—is justly famous, and expresses a common view toward compromise.

The reasons for entering into a compromise are so simple and seemingly obvious that explaining them seems largely unnecessary. Without compromise, legislation is often impossible. People who desire the enactment of legislation and the benefits it provides will be motivated to accept a compromise because, even if it affords less than they would want in the best of all possible worlds, it creates conditions better than would exist in the absence of any agreement. The logic and necessity of compromise are compelling, but there are also several countervailing reasons to avoid compromise. First, it can be hard to explain compromise to enthusiastic constituents. Second, the parties can find it highly beneficial to maintain differences between them. Third, entering into a compromise today can preclude getting more later.

Compromise is so important in politics that scholars and observers of political processes have tended to ignore the importance of disagreement in getting what you want. Hightower's admonition that "there's nothing in the middle of the road but yellow stripes and dead armadillos" represents a common tendency among political activists, to whom compromise is anathema. Exponents of Rayburn's position see themselves as responsible people whose mission it is to make the government work as well as possible, to pass bills that move public policy in a beneficial direction. They accept compromise if the alternative is doing nothing at all, and do not spurn half a loaf. They embrace bipartisanship, not happily, but as the best way to get things done. Opposed to these governance-minded compromisers are the future-oriented Jim Hightowers, who are more concerned with advancing their own and their political party's electoral prospects and with putting forward an alternative political agenda. They are less interested in implementing piecemeal solutions to problems today than in framing clear choices for the electorate and ensuring that responsibility is allocated clearly, so that they can triumph in the next election and then implement their program. They hold out for the whole loaf.

A dispute in 1959 between Senate Majority Leader Lyndon Johnson and the Democratic Advisory Council articulated the strategic differences with admirable clarity. As a strongly Democratic Congress with an ambitious agenda faced a conservative Republican president, the Democratic Advisory Council made a classic argument for purity over compromise:

> The record should be clearly written. The Congress should not be intimidated by threats of Presidential veto. The American people are entitled to have the lines definitely drawn.
>
> It is our considered judgment that the interests of the nation and the people would be best served by passing the legislation the Democratic majority knows the country needs, and by putting it into the President's hands to sign or veto. . . . When and if bills are vetoed, the differences between the Democratic and Republican parties would be even more sharply brought into focus so that voters will understand them in the election of 1960.[3]

Lyndon Johnson spoke for the virtues of compromise:

> In a government which is divided, we can either do something or do nothing. . . .
>
> I think the Senate has acted wisely. I think it has demonstrated that it is reasonable and fair, that it is not hard headed, that it is not adopting a "me too" attitude. It believes that if we cannot do all we desire to do, we should at least do what can be done. . . . We can either do something or nothing. As for myself, speaking for the party I attempt to represent, I prefer to do something.[4]

Lyndon Johnson and the Limits of Conciliation
Lyndon Johnson is the exemplar of compromise in American politics, rising, on the strength of his ability to forge a compromise, to

become the most powerful Senate leader of the century. His experience shows both the advantages and disadvantages of a preference for compromise. He was called a legislative genius and celebrated for his finagling in the Senate. Johnson believed that "in an era of national conciliation," the road to Democratic political success was "paved with modest bills actually passed [and not with] proposals that could not be enacted."[5] He was averse to having the Democrats labelled "big spenders" by the Republicans, which they invariably would be if they passed a flood of legislation that called for new expenditures. He also feared that passing bills the president would veto would open them to charges of extreme partisanship. It would appear they were "tormenting the benign and well-loved war hero in the White House."[6] On the other side were liberals who found bipartisanship frustrating, and who believed they could best advance themselves and their party by writing and passing uncompromising legislation that truly reflected their views. If President Eisenhower vetoed these bills, it would only strengthen Democrats' chances of winning the White House in 1960. As liberal strength grew over the 1950s, so too did the ability of liberals to force confrontation, and the number of vetoes issued by President Eisenhower reached a peak. Johnson's pragmatic political orientation came under severe assault, even before Rayburn and Johnson left Congress, from liberal Democrats who believed it was better to have no legislation than to pass the "watered-down" compromise legislation possible with Eisenhower as president. Especially after the 1958 congressional elections, an enlarged liberal wing of the Democratic party pressured the leadership to act on liberal initiatives, even when there was no hope of them becoming law. Paul Butler, Democratic party chairman, wanted "more partisan fire" in Congress and believed that Johnson "spent too much time in worrying about unity and not enough in probing the opposition's weaknesses."[7]

Johnson wanted to be elected president, but was beat out for the Democratic nomination by Senator John Kennedy, who had virtually no legislative achievements to his name. In a political environment where advancement depends on mobilizing an army of supporters, clear articulation of policy counts more than the ability to cut a deal.[8] Deal makers win the respect of insiders, but their skills will be generally unappreciated outside elite circles. Kennedy specialized in espousing policy, whereas Johnson concerned himself with passing what legislation he could, even if it was modest. Harry McPherson writes that after 1958 the liberals in Congress

> wished to mount an ideological offensive that would set the terms for the coming election. As before, Johnson preferred trimming reluctantly to failing proudly. Obviously he [Johnson] would run [for president] as a "can-do" leader, whose negotiating skills would transfer easily to the White House. [But] his calls for moderation and nonpartisanship, while winning "independent" support, offended the hot partisans who cast a major share of the votes at every Democratic convention—and one had to win there, before taking advantage of independent support in the country.[9]

Compromise is often of negligible value in winning friends. Johnson's greatest legislative achievement as Senate leader was the passage of the 1957 Civil Rights Act—the first civil rights measure passed in eighty-two years. Yet this extraordinary achievement was greeted with mixed reaction from the civil rights community, many of whose members opposed its passage because it had been greatly watered down to get it passed. Lyndon Johnson was determined to obtain passage of a civil rights bill in 1957, believing it necessary to his aspirations for national political office. All through his previous political career he had, as a Texan, voted dutifully against all civil rights legislation.[10] To gain stature among his fellow Democrats and to prove he was not just a regional politician, he sought to do what no liberals had been able to do: pass civil rights legislation. But at the same time he had to avoid a split in the Democratic party and prevent a filibuster.

Somehow, he managed to pull off this "miracle," as Evans and Novak described it. Ironically, although passing the bill may have proved he was not a segregationist, it did not gain him the kind of support needed to win the Democratic nomination. Johnson engineered two key compromises with Senator Richard Russell, Democrat of Georgia and leader of the southern delegation, who promised in exchange to suppress a filibuster. The first was the deletion of Title III, which concerned school desegregation. The second compromise was the institution of jury trials for persons cited for contempt of court in civil rights cases. Since white juries were expected to acquit all persons so charged, the jury trial provision would effectively nullify all voting rights provisions in the bill. Johnson supported floor amendments in the Senate to effect both changes, and deployed his formidable skills to obtain their passage.[11]

Liberals felt cheated by the compromises that made passage possible, and Southerners began to think that Johnson was not one of them. Certainly nothing would have satisfied both the Southerners and northern liberals, but Johnson's course of action gained him no enthusiastic following and made him suspect to civil rights liberals and conservatives alike.

These compromises emptied the passage of the civil rights bill of nearly all but symbolic meaning, and thus deprived Johnson's personal victory in passing it of much substantive importance. Only the weaker bill had a chance of actually becoming law and therefore Johnson, ever the practical politician, worked for the weaker bill. If strong voting rights language had somehow survived the jury trial amendment, sure death awaited it at the hands of a southern filibuster. But to many, the weaker bill was not worth having. Ralph Bunche and A. Phillip Randolph thought the bill in its weakened form was possibly worse than none at all. After first hesitating, both Roy Wilkins and Martin Luther King, Jr. came out for the bill; they met criticism from leading black newspapers. Joseph Rauh opposed the bill. Senator Paul Douglas likened the bill to "soup made from the shadow of a crow which had starved to death."[12]

To many civil rights activists, a strong bill that failed because of a southern filibuster might very well have been preferable to a neutered bill that passed. According to Evans and Novak, had the Southerners used a filibuster to kill the civil rights bill, the national response would have been such outrage that the filibuster itself would have been threatened.[13] This is implausible, but enthusiasts probably hoped for and expected such an outcome, and being deprived of the opportunity to fight their case on the public stage must have been a disappointment.

What did passage of the civil rights bill do for Johnson? Enactment of the Civil Rights Act of 1957 was hailed as a great achievement by the New York Times, which called it "incomparably the most significant domestic action of any Congress in this century."[14] Given that the actual achievements of the legislation itself were close to nil, this sort of praise seems overblown, but it reflects the surprise of contemporary observers that such legislation could pass, and indicates the level of respect as a legislative leader Johnson earned among elite observers. Johnson convinced all watchers that he was indeed a legislative wizard—the most powerful Senate leader of the twentieth century. He also demonstrated that he was not a segregationist, and this relieved his presidential aspirations of an impossible burden. The civil rights bill did not encourage any group to support Johnson, however. In the eyes of Southerners, previously his strongest supporters, he must have become suspect on the question of civil rights. Civil rights leaders, for the most part disappointed with the final, pale version of the bill, were not won over either. The constituency that most appreciated Johnson's accomplishments were journalists, politicians, and other close observers of the Senate, who, however, could not form the basis of a presidential campaign.

What are the overall political prospects of a compromiser in national politics? For every issue on which Johnson managed to pass a bill by reaching a compromise that did serious damage to the bill (in the eyes of its strongest supporters), Johnson at least partially alienated a constituency. To the extent that advancement in national politics depends on mobilizing the support of enthusiastic constituencies, practicing compromise and accommodation hinder a candidate.

The pragmatic orientation has frequently hurt congressional leaders, particularly Republicans, sometimes causing their demise. This was a lesson that Senator Bob Dole, Republican of Kansas, learned in the 1988 presidential campaign. He was majority leader for six years under President Reagan at a time when the budget deficit soared. As majority leader he sought to fashion compromise legislation to cut the deficit, which necessarily included tax increases. Many observers of Congress saw him as a pragmatic figure who did what was required to combat deficits, but his actions angered conservative Republicans who condemned him as the "taxman for the welfare state," and served as a serious impediment to his presidential ambitions in 1988. In the New Hampshire primary in 1988, George Bush revived his failing presidential campaign by attacking Dole on the tax issue, calling Dole a "straddler" who sometimes favored and sometimes opposed tax increases. By contrast, Bush portrayed himself as pure in his opposition to taxes.[15]

Other compromisers have met similar fates. Representative Joe Martin, Republican of Massachusetts, was ousted as House minority leader by Charles Halleck in 1959, to a large extent because Republicans saw Martin as too cozy with Democrats and because they wanted someone who "would fight for the issues."[16] Charles McNary, Senate Republican minority leader through much of the New Deal period, was sufficiently friendly with Democrats that FDR considered him for a running mate in 1940. McNary played golf and fished with Democratic majority leader Joe Robinson. He was not overthrown, but dissatisfaction with his style of leadership led to the elevation of Robert Taft, a ferocious partisan warrior, as the informal leader of Senate Republicans, after McNary became ill and retired.[17]

The congressional leaders with the most exalted reputations among elites have been those gifted at deal making, able and willing to strike a deal in order to move legislation. Yet while such leaders have received the praise of the media and of academic critics, their efforts to forge compromise and pass laws have hurt their efforts to win higher office, and have frequently complicated relations with their own party.

Reasons Not to Compromise

The success of Newt Gingrich in rising through the Republican party in the House of Representatives illustrates some of the reasons to avoid compromise. Gingrich and some other conservative Republicans in Congress contended that the best way for Republicans to win a majority in Congress was to confront and challenge Democrats at every opportunity in order to distinguish clearly between the parties. Cooperating with Democrats on the enactment of legislation may have produced slightly better bills in the short term, but hindered efforts to win the big prize—Republican majorities in Congress. The 1994 congressional elections, which gave Republicans their first majority in the House of Representatives in forty years, appear to have vindicated Gingrich's staunchly partisan tactics. Similarly, the Democrats who controlled Congress had frequent opportunities to engage in negotiations and compromise with Republican presidents. Some Democrats saw compromise as the only way to produce legislation, when control of the national government was divided between parties, but others took the view that negotiations with Republican presidents were for the most part a hindrance to efforts to put a Democrat in the White House.[18]

Despite the frequency of compromise as a means of resolving legislative disagreement confrontation, and the deliberate avoidance of agreement are also extremely common and important ways of dealing with policy disputes. Politicians routinely exhibit behavior that in normal bargaining situations would seem bizarre. When the other side makes a major concession, they may respond by increasing their demand; they may prefer no agreement to a compromise that is a clear improvement over the status quo; and they may actually move apart rather than closer together over the course of a negotiation. The explanation for apparently perverse bargaining is that politicians often prefer disagreement to agreement, believing that the compromises necessary to reach an agreement may be more politically damaging than no agreement at all.

Collectively, we will call these tactics strategies of disagreement; they manifest themselves in a wide variety of circumstances. In general, stragegies of disagreement are most likely to be employed when politicians deal with issues that appeal to and excite large constituencies, and when politicians compete for the support of these constituencies. Under divided government, when the president and Congress are in a continual battle, strategies of disagreement are particularly useful and commonly employed. When senators compete, either with each other or with an incumbent president, for a presidential nomination, they also find disagreement useful. Finally, interest groups that need a crisis to generate memberships may prefer to avoid an agreement.

Problems of Explanation

The fundamental problem in explaining compromises may be summarized as follows: first, politicians are interested not just in advancing the interests of constituents, but also in retaining their offices; second, constituents may fail to recognize a compromise as the best that can be gotten under the circumstances and may confuse it with betrayal. Consequently, it is not always in the best electoral interest of politicians to obtain moderate improvements in the status quo. In negotiations, the parties must concern themselves not just with reaching an agreement that is an improvement over the status quo, but also with being able to convince their supporters that it is an advance.

A fundamental political problem that renders compromise so difficult is the near impossibility of explaining decisions about extremely complex issues to audiences that pay virtually no attention to politics. When dealing with policy issues that involve mass constituencies and "expressive" interest groups, politicians who seek the support of those constituencies must worry that the constituencies will mistake compromise for betrayal. They must be concerned about interest group leaders and rival politicians who have incentives to portray compromises as sellouts of constituencies. The difficulty of explaining complex choices to inattentive audiences leads politicians to take only actions that can be easily explained, and which are not subject to deliberate distortion by rivals.

Elite negotiators know far more than their constituents and followers, and this has a vast impact on the course of bargaining. Members of Congress and executive branch officials vary in their understanding of policy, but they are much more sophisticated than ordinary voters. An important part of this sophistication is an understanding of political feasibility. They are more likely than members of the mass public to understand that divided party control of the government, factionalization of the parties, and the multitude of impediments to simple majority rule mean that neither side can get its way entirely in contentious issues, and that compromise is necessary to get legislation passed. In addition, political elites know the preferences and constraints of their bargaining partners, which makes it possible for them to predict the range of settlements acceptable to their partner. Democrats understand that a Republican president has certain constraints about agreeing to tax increases, while Republicans understand that Democrats are more than a little touchy about Social Security. Suppose, for the sake of argument, that a politician has negotiated the best possible deal for his constituents. He and other well-informed observers will know that this is the best possible deal because they understand the political system and the constellation of opposing political forces that limit the range of possible agreements.

The participants in the negotiations, however, are responsible to other groups and individuals in the mass arena whose lives and fortunes are likely to be affected, but who are not sophisticated. They do not have a good understanding either of the problem or of the political circumstances surrounding it, and are thus far less aware than the politicians of the necessity of compromise. Consequently, the mass audience can readily interpret a compromise that hurts them as a sellout. Explaining otherwise requires educating constituents, not an easy task. Richard Fenno views "education" as any explanation of Washington activity that at least "hurts a little." In his journeys with eighteen members of Congress he found almost no willingness for members of Congress to expend even a little political capital on the education of constituents.[19]

Educating inattentive constituents is never easy, but it is made immeasurably more difficult by the presence of other, rival leaders who seek to advance their own interests by criticizing compromises. Competing politicians who are not party to the negotiations can attempt to gain favor by charging that the compromise was not necessary and that the problem could have been solved without sacrificing the interests of the audience. Whom are the constituents to believe? Much will depend on the persuasiveness of the critic and the credibility of the incumbent politician. But certainly politicians must dread returning to their supporters to defend half a loaf. The critic of the compromise conveys a message that people want to hear—that they can have what they want—while the defender must bring bad news. The critic has a simple message to convey—"they're selling you out!"—while the defender has a complex message—"we had to agree to this admittedly unsatisfactory compromise because of circumstances beyond our control." The difficulties and risks of selling an unattractive compromise agreement to an unsophisticated mass audience can prevent the emergence of such an agreement.

Voters are susceptible to the blandishments of interest groups and rival politicians because they are not themselves well equipped to evaluate the actions of representatives. As Anthony Downs and others have observed, voters are rationally ignorant. They do not acquire a great deal of information because they do not find it worth acquiring.[20] Consequently they must depend on judgments borrowed from other authorities, few of whom are objective providers of information. Most voters are only mildly attentive to politics, and perceive little of the complexity of debates on public policy and legislation. They have preferences about policy, but these are ill-focused, generally taking the form of a positive feeling toward environmentalism, health care for the elderly, and other policy topics. They know what they want—a clean environment, say, or better education—but they know little about the means or costs of achieving that goal, or the trade-offs with competing policy goals.[21] Arguments favoring or opposing most public policies imply complex ends-means chains that are often too intricate even for highly attentive people to unravel. Judgments of the electorate toward policies and legislation generally take the form of favorable or unfavorable opinions, and must necessarily be borrowed from newspapers, television, organizations, and politicians, rather than developed through research and cogitation. Few providers of information and opinion are disinterested. Interest group leaders want to increase membership and promote their agenda, politicians want to mobilize support and votes, newspapers want to stimulate readership—and all shape their message and interpretations of events to their purposes.

The interest groups of concern here are those described by Robert Salisbury as "expressive," meaning that people join them not just to achieve a purpose, but to express a view. An important return that members get from their contribution is knowing they have supported the expression of values they believe in.[22] Examples of expressive groups are Common Cause, Ralph Nader's constellation of groups, various environmental groups, ideological groups, and so on. Several observations about these groups are in order. First, many such groups are insecure, and maintaining their membership is a vital concern. Second, the members tend to be enthusiastic about the cause. Third, because such groups are inexpensive to organize, they are subject to factionalization. "A rival to the leadership needs only a membership list and a better line to support a factional fight."[23]

Participants in such groups are often "purists,"[24] and for many purists a compromise is a betrayal. "Purists are honest but a pain in the ass," Hubert H. Humphrey is reported to have said.[25] Peggy Noonan writes about the "movement conservatives" in the Reagan years who were unwilling to tolerate any deviation from the true line. They were, she said, "a bunch of creepy little men with creepy little beards who need something to seethe on (State Department cookie-pushers! George Bush! The Trilateral Commission!). . . . These are not people who mourn when someone disappoints them, they like it. More proof of human perfidy! More proof of the ugliness at the core of the human heart!"[26] Expressive interest groups are motivated to retain and gain members and they do this by staking out positions and making claims that will move people to open their checkbooks. The language of moderation and compromise does not appear to generate many memberships.[27]

Leaders of expressive groups sometimes cannot back compromise without endangering their memberships or inviting a schism. This is a serious problem of political organization, creating a contest between maintaining an organization and achieving goals through the political process. As Jane Mansbridge explains in the context of the ERA fight, "To change the world, a movement must include as many people as possible. But to attract devoted activists, a movement must promote a sense of exclusivity—'we happy few, we band of brothers.' "[28] Political parties also have this problem in that their most enthusiastic members, who do much of the difficult work, are not representative of the larger group the party wants to attract as voters.[29]

Within both interest groups and political parties, rivalries for leadership tend to discourage moderation. Because expressive groups are inexpensive to build, rival organizations are relatively easy to create. Ambitious entrepreneurs can take advantage of moderation among a group's leaders to denounce them for betraying the interests of the group, and establish their own, new organizations on correct principles. Borrowing the mailing list of the parent organization, the new schismatic organization may steal away many of the more hot-blooded members. Unless a group is sure of its members' loyalties, moderation can be dangerous.[30] Similarly, ambitious members of a political party can use moderate speech and actions among the leaders to advance their own cause. A president or party leader who agrees to a compromise inevitably transgresses one article or another of the true faith, causing a Newt Gingrich or his functional equivalent to rise up and point out the preacher's sins, offering to take the tainted leader's place.

Daniel P. Moynihan wrote of the National Welfare Rights Organization (NWRO), which, in its efforts to block welfare reforms to which it was opposed, attacked liberals who supported Nixon's Family Assistance Plan. "NWRO's tactics came close to a policy of punishing friends and rewarding enemies: a portent of short organizational life."[31] Despite Moynihan's dim view of such tactics, they are widely practiced. Nor do such organizations necessarily have a short life. In 1970 Senator Edmund Muskie found himself the object of an attack by Ralph Nader and an affiliated group for his environmental record. Muskie was the leading candidate for the Democratic nomination in 1972, no doubt partly because he was generally considered the leading environmental senator. This identity, in the minds of the public and political activists, was enormously valuable to Muskie. So when a Ralph Nader group issued a report that attacked Muskie's environmental credentials, it was a major blow.[32] A record that had been unambiguously pro-environmental suddenly became doubtful. Muskie's response was to go on an environmental offensive that

erased any questions surrounding his credentials. Muskie had no af-
fection for the Nader group but he did what they wanted. Twenty
years later, when a new clean air law was being written, environmentalists again attacked allies who seemed inclined toward compromise.[33] Representative John Dingell claimed that environmentalists
did not even want to pass a bill, but preferred to hold onto the issue:
"They were like Irishmen at a wake. They wanted to keep the party
going forever."[34] In 1989, as Congress considered legislation to fund
day care, Marion Wright Edelman, a leading children's rights advocate, launched a bitter attack on two members of the House who
proposed alternative legislation, despite their having been among
Edelman's strongest supporters in the past.[35] There may be the same
tendency on the right to attack political figures that are ideologically
close rather than far away. Senator Milton Young of North Dakota
complained about the anticommunist John Birch Society: "Strangely
enough, most of its criticism is leveled, not against liberal public officials, but against the middle-of-the-road, and even conservative,
Republicans."[36] These attacks discourage trust and may preclude a
fruitful collaborative relationship. Instead of trust, they inspire a
sense of fear and loathing which, in its own way, can be very useful,
since the expectation of being attacked may dissuade politicians from
veering away from an orthodoxy. Shrewd politicians understand
which groups they cannot afford to alienate and act accordingly.

Attacking one's enemies might seem on the surface to make more
sense, and it is done, but it tends to have less effect because the ob-
jects of the attack do not mind and may even enjoy being attacked.
When the NWRO staged a sit-in of the Senate Finance Committee,
"the term 'Black Brood Mares, Inc.' was coined, and ascribed to Russell Long. . . . It enjoyed a wide currency. Thereafter Long's office
tended to be left alone."[37] Attacks on friends can be effective in bringing them in line on important issues, because friends may need a
group's endorsement. The withdrawal of support is what groups can
use as a threat and this threat leaves enemies unconcerned.

Expressive groups can gain power far beyond what their membership rosters might suggest, because through their endorsements or denunciations they can help to validate or invalidate candidates' claims about their achievements and positions. Any candidate can say that he or she is an environmentalist, but only some candidates can get the endorsement of the Sierra Club or other environmental groups. To the extent that candidates value affiliations with expressive groups or fear their criticism, they must give voice to the views the groups embrace and avoid actions the groups would disparage.[38]

The second disincentive to compromise stems from competition within a party. A politician who consents to a compromise often comes under attack from rivals within his own party for having sold out the interests of constituents. By its very nature, a compromise does not deliver all that constituents want. Nonetheless, it probably represents a net gain for the constituents. A politician who makes himself party to a compromise is open to the criticism, from other politicians seeking to curry favor with the constituency, that he has sold out the interests of the group. Whether or not this is true is somewhat irrelevant, for if constituents are unaware of the necessity of a compromise, they are subject to manipulation by other politicians who can take advantage of the difficulty of explaining compromise. Bush happily attacked Dole for his willingness to raise taxes, never bothering to explain that these were almost exclusively tax increases that President Reagan had agreed to as well.

Solutions and agreements that make sense at the elite level, but which cannot be explained well at the mass level, create opportunities for politicians to gain an audience by attacking those who made the agreement. Two episodes from recent years indicate the near impossibility of communicating the real circumstances when a politician or interest group is intent on disseminating misleading interpretations. The first of these is the Social Security "notch." Congress adopted legislation that seemed to make sense to an elite audience, but which could be manipulated and misrepresented to mass audiences in ways that were difficult to rebut. The notch has been a continuing nightmare to responsible politicians and a great opportunity for the unscrupulous. The second instance is the effort to withhold taxes from interest and dividend income. These interesting cases illustrate the immense difficulty politicians can face in explaining complex issues to inattentive voters when other elites are determined to spread misinformation. An asymmetry exists whereby it is harder to correct erroneous, simplistic beliefs than to plant them initially.

The so-called Social Security notch was created by Congress in 1977 when it was forced to correct a formula for calculating cost-of-living allowances that produced excessively large benefit increases. To avoid the political difficulties of taking back benefits from those who had gotten unreasonably large increases, Congress decided to "grandfather" those who had already received the windfall. Consequently, there is a sudden change in benefit levels—a notch—and most people who were born between 1917 and 1921 receive lower Social Security benefits than individuals born a few years earlier.[39] The disparity is unfair, if judged by the standard that like cases ought to be treated alike. But the situation is not as unfair as it might seem on the surface, because the notch victims themselves get larger benefits than retirees born later. This is a complex problem, but one that a Social Security expert could probably explain to the satisfaction of most notch babies, if given a few uninterrupted minutes. But it is difficult to get anyone's attention for that long.

Political entrepreneurs can readily communicate the injustice to victims by means of dramatic graphic displays revealing higher benefits for the earlier retirees and lower benefits for their immediate successors.[40] Such entrepreneurs invariably fail to convey the full complexity of the issue, since their intent is to arouse the anger of the audience. The leading notch issue agitator is the National Committee to Preserve Social Security and Medicare, founded by James Roosevelt. This group, which has a history of using scare tactics to convince senior citizens to join,[41] has sent out mailings on the issue to its 5 million members, and has provided money and logistical support to notch groups in several states.[42] Roosevelt's group works with a very effective direct mail firm that is known for writing "provocative copy." Discussing the committee's mailings, a direct mail consultant explained that informed people "will laugh at it, but to [the uninformed people Roosevelt's group targets], this is righteous, moral shit. This is table pounding stuff."[43]

Most politicians have neither time nor incentive to convince a group of agitated, table-pounding notch babies that they deserve no compensation. Taking on the issue in a serious way would primarily expose a senator or representative to abuse from senior groups and would consume a lot of time. Members of Congress would normally be inclined to correct the notch,[44] except that proposed remedies cost between $24 billion and $300 billion—money that is unavailable. Instead of addressing this "issue from hell," most congressmen ignore it as much as possible, commission studies when they cannot,[45] and hope that it will go away. But Roosevelt's National Commission can solicit memberships by talking about the notch, and members of Congress can seek votes and support by promising to fix it, all of which serves to heighten and confirm the notch babies' sense of injustice, continually giving new life to an issue that should have been disposed of long ago.

The effort to introduce withholding of federal taxes on interest and dividend income provides another example of entrepreneurial exploitation of voter ignorance. In 1982 Congress was faced with an exploding federal deficit and sought to reduce it in ways that were relatively painless politically. One such route was to increase tax revenues by improving collection. Since collection is far better when the tax is withheld at its source, Congress tried to introduce withholding of taxes for interest and dividends in the Tax Equity and Fiscal Responsibility Act of 1982 (TEFRA). Most informed observers would see nothing terribly controversial in an effort to crack down on tax cheats. But they would be wrong, at least in this case.

The problem was that withholding imposed a burden of paper-work that was troubling, especially to smaller banks. TEFRA moved too quickly through Congress for these banks to mount an effective campaign against its initial enactment, but their response was devastating.

With Senator Bob Kasten, Republican of Wisconsin, as their leader in Congress, the financial industries began a campaign of misinformation to convince depositors to resist withholding. Joseph White and Aaron Wildavsky write that banks

> claimed it would cost $1.5 billion to administer the 10-percent withholding of interest on their accounts. Although that fact explained their concern, it was no way to mobilize voter pressure on Congress; instead bankers told their customers that the government was going to take their money away. A sample speech declared that withholding would "loot your savings account." One ad led off in large boldface type: "Warning: 10 percent of the money you earn in interest is going to disappear"—with the word "disappear" fading to white.[46]

This misrepresentation of the real nature of tax withholding was magnificently successful. Banks sent out some 80 million postcards for their customers to send to members of Congress. About 4 million were mailed in, creating the largest mail campaign to Congress ever. The congressional leadership of both parties tried to stop the repeal effort, but they were unsuccessful in the face of a complete panic among their followers. In the House a discharge petition forced a bill out of committee, and in the Senate Kasten offered a repeal amendment to unrelated legislation. The banking forces won in a rout, and the law was repealed in 1983.[47]

An astonishing feature of the repeal effort is that many of its proponents—bank customers, that is, not banks—believed they were fighting a new tax. Conceivably, members of Congress could have embarked on a campaign of clarification and convinced depositors of the truth, that this was simply a new way of collecting an old tax that would reduce tax evasion. But how would a representative go about conducting this campaign? Take out ads on television or write letters to all people who had gotten misleading information from the banks? This would take a great deal of time, effort, and money, and in the end would probably be only slightly successful. It was worthwhile for the banks to engage in their campaign of misinformation, but not for supporters of the law to fight the bankers. So members of Congress took the easier course and backed down.

Politicians are often compelled to emulate the inflexibility of zealots, or to act as if they were no more sophisticated than gullible constituents. The problem of explaining their choices and actions to the public is vastly complicated by the willingness—even eagerness—of rival politicians and ambitious interest group leaders to present alternative, possibly misleading explanations. When a member of Congress votes for a pay raise, an increase in the debt ceiling, a cut in spending, or an increase in taxes, or when he or she reaches a compromise with leaders of the other party, some may see this as statesmanlike behavior, making hard choices that involve risks. From the viewpoint of aspiring representatives, however, such choices look for the most part like opportunities for launching a campaign to unseat the incumbent. All these votes can in principle be explained by the representative, but the explanation usually requires at least several sentences or paragraphs; an attack on these positions can be launched and completed much more quickly. In cases where one side of a controversial issue requires a more complicated explanation, politicians must consider carefully whether they will be able to convey their reasons to the public. R. Douglas Arnold considers the calculations of representatives and argues they are adept at anticipating the "potential preferences" of their constituents, which means understanding the kinds of votes and positions that will open them to criticism from rivals. They avoid taking positions they cannot readily explain.[48]

Group leaders and elected officials often must act as if their understanding of politics and policy were no more sophisticated than that of their typically ill-informed constituents. They cannot take actions that are sensible and beneficial if those actions could be misrepresented to their publics by rival leaders or interest groups. This is quite the reverse of what was intended by the authors of the Constitution, who had hoped that each stage of political selection would refine and improve public opinion. In most cases the political process does produce elected officials who are more intelligent and thoughtful than the general public, but the susceptibility of the public to mis- and disinformation means that elected officials often cannot act on their own best judgment.

It's Good to Maintain Distance Between the Parties

When politicians enter into compromise agreements with their competitors, they allow legislation to pass, but they also sacrifice the opportunity to criticize their opponents. When Democrats and Republicans reach an agreement on an issue of interest to large numbers of constituents, there is no reason for the constituents to prefer one party over the other. A party or faction that has a position on an issue that attracts votes, and that enjoys an advantage over an opponent, may be reluctant to sacrifice that advantage by accepting a compromise.

A party or faction that is disadvantaged on an important issue will be eager for a compromise as a way of evening things out. Ideally, the best way to eliminate an opponent's advantage is to adopt his or her position, but this approach is often impossible. Politicians are commonly constrained in what they can agree to by previous commitments, by ideology, and by their coalition. Republicans might like to eliminate contemporary Democratic advantages in the health issue, but they cannot match Democratic calls for dramatic solutions because their party stands against such socialistic schemes, and because endorsing Democratic proposals would alienate other Republican constituencies.

Republicans may reach out to Democrats, hoping for a compromise that will be acceptable to their constituents, but the Democrats will not offer their hand. If they do reach a compromise, the differences between the parties, formerly clear, are blurred. Voters and activists who preferred Democrats because of the health issue have no further reason to prefer Democrats over Republicans. Thus Democrats have good reason to avoid compromise. Efforts to reach a compromise can undermine efforts to win elections. If the electorate were perfectly informed about the political situation, they would understand that the compromise was the best they could get and realize that one party really would like to do more for them, but cannot under the circumstances. They would understand that their party is doing the best it can, and that if it gained full control of the government it would be better able to satisfy constituents' demands. But constituencies being what they are, and politicians and interest groups being what they are, such an explanation is difficult to convey. Politicians often believe that the best way to obtain the support and loyalty of voters is to highlight differences.

If the Democrats have an advantage over the Republicans in an issue—health, say—and the Republicans believe their position hurts them, a natural Republican response would be to propose health legislation. Even if the legislation does not pass, they can say they have a bill, a plan, and are interested in the issue. Legislation may not pass, but at least they can introduce ambiguity over who is in favor of what in the health field. Perhaps the best thing of all for the Republicans is to lure the Democrats into passing a meager health bill. Then the Republicans have given up little, but can still say there is no difference between the parties. Democrats understand that the Republicans will try to offset their advantage in the health field, and they are far from helpless. As the Republicans move strategically toward the Democratic position, the Democrats move strategically away. If they can avoid an agreement, they may preserve their primacy in the issue.

Another important political advantage of stridency stems from the importance of factions and activists in the modern presidential campaign. As political parties have weakened organizationally, candidates have been forced to rely increasingly on organized interests to run their campaigns. Candidates and parties that do not stimulate enthusiasm among organized interests can suffer. In the 1976 presidential campaign, Jimmy Carter promised to create a department of education. The National Education Association went all out to help Carter win, and apparently their assistance was immensely helpful. A willingness to engage in compromise is unlikely to generate campaign support.

Consenting to an agreement can diminish future electoral prospects by reducing or eliminating issue advantages. Conversely, partisan electioneering and the bashing of one's opponents can diminish the likelihood of success in elite negotiations, because attacks on one's opponents may make them wary of further negotiations. A keen awareness among politicians of the connections between efforts to garner political support and efforts to reach compromises to pass legislation exerts an important influence on the conduct of negotiations. The requirements of building and maintaining an electoral coalition in the mass arena complicate efforts to reach a compromise in the elite arena. When, for example, a presidential candidate swears he will never allow taxes to be raised, that may help him to be elected, but it limits his freedom to bargain once in office. Conversely, agreeing in elite negotiations to Social Security spending cuts may forever alienate an important constituency. Politicians are thus in a perpetual conflict between the needs of governing, which require compromise, and those of wooing electoral support, which discourage it.

There has been substantial academic discussion of party strategies and whether they diverge or converge on issues. In the Downsian world of political competition, they converge.[49] If one party is thought to have a superior position on an important issue, the other party will simply adopt that position. Both parties move to the same point as the median voter. The party with an advantage on an issue will not respond to the incursion of its opponent because it already occupies the best possible position. Some significant attributes of Downs's political world make such a result logical. First, parties are unconstrained by constituency ties: they always adopt whatever position will get them the most votes and do not worry that shifting their position and offending a previously loyal constituency will have any cost. Second, voters perceive the party positions with a good deal of clarity. This point caused Downs some difficulty, for he recognized the problem of rational ignorance among voters, and spent several tortured and not very successful chapters explaining how voters could economically but accurately learn the positions of parties.[50]

Subsequent research recognized that, in the real world of politics, parties are commonly observed to diverge; it sought to explain why parties would not converge on the median voter. Benjamin I. Page showed empirically patterns of both convergence and divergence. On some issues the parties do converge on a point preferred by voters while on others they diverge and take position at odds with those of voters.[51] Thomas Palfrey has conjectured that parties distance themselves in order to prevent entry from other political parties.[52]

In this book I show a number of patterns of convergence and divergence. One party will often try to converge and the other will simultaneously diverge. One party will try to reduce its disadvantage by converging and the other will try to maintain its advantage by diverging. From the standpoint of a spatial analysis of party politics, such strategies do not make sense because the party diverging should already have occupied the position that yields the most votes. Moving away from that point only loses them votes.

The strategy of diverging and maintaining distinctiveness in response to concessions of an opponent does make sense, however, if voters are unsophisticated. Individuals have preferences about policy, but because of their lack of knowledge and sophistication, these preferences do not map well onto the policy space. Parties and politicians do not choose policies based on a calculation that a particular policy is closest to the electorate, but rather in an attempt to position themselves attractively in relation to the opponent. Rationally ignorant voters will not know precisely where a party stands on a particular issue, but they will be able to identify differences between parties, and know, for example, that one stands for more and the other for less.[53] On health care issues, the Democrats want to be the party promising more than the Republicans. On crime, the Republicans want to be the party that is tougher on criminals. Exact positions in policy space are less important than relative positions because voters cannot perceive exact positions of parties, only relative positions.

Accepting Half a Loaf Now May Prevent Getting More Later

Politicians may also be reluctant to enter into compromises because a compromise today may preclude a total victory later. When the Democrats control Congress but a Republican inhabits the White House, legislation can often pass only if watered down. But suppose that the Democrats expect they have a good chance of winning the next presidential election. If they wait, they may be able to pass the legislation in a stronger form. This reason for avoiding compromise can be entirely rational and in the best long-term interest of constituents.

Issue advocates are often reluctant to accept a compromise because they hope that, even if they cannot get their preferred bill now, at least they can force a presidential veto, which will indicate in the clearest possible terms the positions of the two parties. Advocates often anticipate that having the party differences so clearly displayed will help them win in the next election, after which they will be able to enact an unadulterated form of the bill. From this perspective, compromises now diminish future electoral prospects, and reduce the likelihood of future policy victories. The uncompromising perspective in politics is often summarized: "If we don't get a bill, at least we will still have an issue." At any one time it may be necessary to choose between a bill and an issue, but those who are patient (and lucky) can get the political benefits from the issue today, and pass the ideal bill later. Compromise today may undermine chances of winning in the next election and put off the day of complete policy victory.

There are numerous instances of policy activists subverting a middle-of-the-road policy because they believe compromise will prevent enactment of their preferred policy. The strongest supporters of increases in the minimum wage, for example, opposed increases in the earned income tax credit in 1989, even though the tax credit increases real income for low-wage workers. Why? Because "a lot of liberals regard the tax credit as a lever to derail the option they prefer, the minimum wage increase."[54] Some advocates of fundamental health care reform expressed relief that low cost, bare-bones health plans offered by insurance companies in the early 1990s proved unpopular; if they had taken hold, the need for more fundamental changes in the structure of health insurance would have declined.[55] There was a chance to pass a clean air bill in 1988, but Representative Henry Waxman, Democrat of California, and other environmentalists in Congress killed this effort, because they preferred to wait until after the presidential election, when they expected to be able to pass a stronger bill. It was uniformly expected that whoever succeeded Reagan as president would be more favorable toward environmental legislation.[56] In 1960 the National Education Association, anticipating it would do better after the presidential election, preferred no federal aid to education bill to one that provided only construction assistance without aid for teachers' salaries. "If they settled for a half-a-loaf construction bill, many years might elapse before they would have another chance as favorable for aid to salaries."[57] In 1961 Senator Wayne Morse, who wanted to eliminate the filibuster altogether, opposed reducing the threshold for invoking cloture from two-thirds to three-fifths. "If we adopt the 60 percent proposal in this session of Congress," he argued, "we may never get a majority rule in our lifetime. If we get beaten on the majority rule principle, then let us try again and again and again, until we win out."[58]

In a more extreme and harrowing instance of the same strategy, the Shining Path rebels of Peru began a campaign of disrupting "aid programs that offered succor to some of Peru's poorest inhabitants. The rebels' hope is that the poor will embrace their cause, even though the terror campaign is making their lives more miserable."[59] The Shining Path must expect that the worse things are, the stronger the appeal of revolutionary change.

It is improbable that members of Congress would actually try to make things worse in order to adopt a proposal closer to their true preference. A proponent of Medicare, for example, would have trouble explaining why he had voted to reduce federal health care spending. But supporters of Medicare did block the enactment of any increase in Social Security benefits from 1958 to 1965 in order to increase pressure on moderates to support Medicare. Over this period Democrats refused to allow the enactment of Social Security increases without the adoption of Medicare. As Social Security benefits declined in value, members of Congress who were reluctant to support Medicare must have felt their opposition melt a bit as the pressure to adopt a Social Security increase mounted.

Politicians who deprive their constituents of possible improvements in policy probably need feel little concern that they will be punished by outraged constituents. For constituents to seek retribution in this manner, they must understand what existing policy is and the nature of the compromise rejected. Some constituents, but probably not many, will understand this. A guiding assumption in leading political science work has been that politicians are held accountable for their policy positions, not their actual accomplishments.[60] If this is true, it is more dangerous for a politician to accept a compromise that improves the welfare of constituents than to hold out for more.

There are two objections to the strategy, one ethical and the other strategic. First, one can say that on ethical grounds the confrontational strategy may violate elected officials' fiduciary responsibility to their constituents, by rejecting legislation that would produce real improvements in the welfare of their supporters. But if accepting half a loaf now reduces the likelihood of getting the whole thing later, holding out may advance constituents' interests. They will get more, but it will be deferred for some period of time. In evaluating this strategy, one must apply a discount factor to the presumably larger benefits that will be had in the future. The second objection is that, by pursuing a more cooperative course of action, the Democrats might pass the watered-down legislation now, which would help their constituents somewhat in the short term, and then pass the pure form of the bill when their party wins the White House. The advantage of this strategy is that it does not hold one's own constituents hostage, as the more confrontational strategy does. The disadvantage of the moderate approach is that piecemeal reform may substantially delay enactment of comprehensive reform. Which strategy one should adopt depends both on the distribution of support among factions in the legislature, and on whether circumstances will become more or less favorable to legislation in the future.

By simple spatial analysis, we can examine the strategy of avoiding compromise today in order to get it all later. Thomas Romer and Howard Rosenthal have done important work showing that when the status quo or "reversion point"—the policy that will obtain should no action be taken—is below the policy preferred by the median voter, "the amount voted will exceed the median, increasing as the reversion decreases. Spending will thus depend not only on voter preferences but also on the reversion level."[61] Imagine a government with a Democratic legislature and a Republican president, in which both Congress and the president must approve legislation. Let us further imagine it is widely anticipated that the next election will replace the Republican president with a Democrat, and that the Congress will continue under Democratic control. There already exists a limited health policy, but it is regarded as outdated by a majority and change is likely soon, though opinions vary widely as to how much change is needed. Most of the Democrats prefer sweeping changes, while the president and the Republicans in Congress prefer far more limited change. The president's veto permits him to prevent the enactment of any policy more ambitious than he prefers. Thus, if a law is passed prior to the election, it will be limited in nature, the product of a compromise.

Given the expectation that the president will soon be a Democrat, prudent Democrats may prefer no bill, because enacting a compromise now may prevent getting a more comprehensive bill later. The following simple spatial model shows how. The key intuition is fundamental and well known to leaders of radical movements, namely, that relieving the worst consequences of a problem can let off enough steam to prevent an explosion later. Moderates normally prefer piecemeal or incremental reform; but if given a choice between an awful status quo and a dramatic change, they may be persuaded to accept the big change, if only because their opposition to the status quo requires them to do something. Moderates, who may be motivated to support some change, will lose their enthusiasm once the very worst problems have been even partly addressed. To the extent that they adopt this hypothesis, radicals consider reformers their worst enemy.

Figure 1.1 displays the positions on health care of all seven members of a hypothetical Congress; positions farther to the left indicate support for more health care and positions to the right indicate desire for less. The four legislators toward the left are Democrats, and the three members on the right are Republicans. Democrats, because of their majority, have control over the agenda, allowing them to make proposals. In scenario A, the proposer prefers to enact a policy close to the middle of all Democrats. The point marked "SQ" represents current policy, the status quo. The five members to the right of SQ support increasing health care, and the two to the left oppose it. Presented with a choice between two alternatives, all members prefer the one closest to their own position. The most extreme proposal that a majority of members prefers to the status quo is marked with an "X." Any proposal to the left of X will not pass because member 4 (a Democrat), whose vote is pivotal, prefers SQ. The most ambitious proposal that the president will sign is marked "P." Congress can pass X but the president will veto it, so the Congress must either settle for proposal P or pass no bill at all.

Suppose that Congress passes a law implementing the president's preferred position, P, and it becomes the new status quo. Then a new Democratic president is elected. What are the consequences for the enactment of legislation in the next period? Moving the status quo toward the left shifts X, the most extreme policy that can be adopted, toward the right by an equal amount. Scenario B shows the range of policies that can beat the new status quo. The new president's position exerts no constraint on the Congress, being fairly far

Figure 1.1
The Status Quo and Policy Strategy

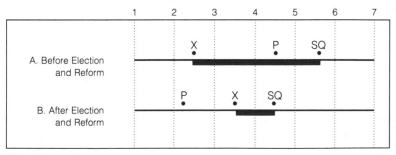

SQ = Status quo
P = President's position
X = most extreme proposal that can win
Heavy line indicates alternatives that beat SQ

to the left. But notice that the distance from SQ to X is much smaller in scenario B than in scenario A. Because the new status quo is quite close to member 4's ideal point, he or she will vote only for minor changes. The farther the status quo diverges from the ideal point of the moderates who must be induced to support changes, the greater the change that can be adopted.[62] But when the urgency of the problem diminishes, only minor changes in the status quo can be implemented.

The liberals have a dilemma. If they know that a Democratic president will win in the next election, it makes sense not to accept P in advance of the election. But the more uncertain they are about the election, the less attractive holding out becomes, because it is possible that a Republican will be elected and that, as a result, the Democrats will be able to get no more after the election than before and will have waited longer to get it.[63] And should they win, the Republicans may also be less inclined to bargain after the election than they were before. It is a difficult calculation.

This logic presents a rationale for policy activists to resist compromise, and for conservatives to embrace moderation. When activists believe that time is on their side, as it surely was in the environmental area in the 1970s, they should hold out for all they want. In the interim, no legislation passes and the status quo is far from their desired point, but they can take comfort in the expectation that soon all will be set right. Conservatives should propose compromises that do not reflect their own views, but which are calculated to forestall future action.

Stalemates and Bidding Wars

What strategies will be adopted by politicians who are unwilling to compromise? What happens when one side wants a compromise but the other does not? The strategy and behavior adopted by politicians will depend very largely on whether the two parties seek to appeal to the same constituency or to different ones, and whether they are trying to hold onto an advantage or erode an opponent's. If both are using an issue to solicit the votes and support of a single group, the likely result will be some form of competitive bidding. On the other hand, if they seek the support of different constituencies, the probable result will be a stalemate.

In stalemates, the two parties to a purported negotiation may move further apart rather than—as one might expect—closer together. When the parties do not seek to capture constituencies from the other side, but rather try to use an issue to solidify their hold on groups already part of their coalition, making concessions may provide no political benefit, and may instead manage only to alienate loyal followers. Normally one might expect that there will be no negotiations when neither side is interested in compromise. But occasionally events and circumstances beyond the control of either party conspire to give an issue extraordinary salience, and the parties must at least pretend to be interested in reaching a compromise, if only to satisfy journalists and other high-minded observers. The ensuing discussions between the parties bear faint resemblance to negotiations, for they typically consist of the issuance of self-serving bargaining positions, and mutual denunciations.

Often a stalemate is not the result of strategic disagreement, but of real disagreement, as when there is no zone of agreement. Stalemates involve strategic disagreement when the two parties are compelled against their will to reach an agreement. This happens when the status quo shifts in such a way that neither party finds it tolerable. For example, in the early 1980s, Social Security teetered on the brink of bankruptcy. If the Social Security trust fund had run out of money and been unable to issue checks, that would have been a political catastrophe of immense proportions. To avoid the catastrophe, compromise between Democrats and Republicans was required, though neither side relished the necessary compromise. Presumably, compromise was superior to bankruptcy, so avoiding that compromise must count as a strategic rather than a real disagreement. Instances of forced negotiations are relatively rare. But under these circumstances, the parties seem to need the cover of secret summit negotiations to overcome the mutual distrust and fear of defection.

Stalemates are comparatively simple phenomena, but when the parties simultaneously use a single issue to appeal to the same group, the strategies multiply. I group these together under the single term "pursuit and avoidance." The basic ploy is for one party, usually (but not always) the Republicans, to try to reduce the political advantage the Democrats have with a constituency by coming close to, matching, or exceeding the Democrats' promises.[64] Rather than allow the Republicans to steal the issue, for example, Democrats respond by increasing their promises. In this scenario, the Republicans want a compromise agreement and the Democrats do their best to prevent one. Unless the Republicans are especially dogged in their pursuit of an agreement, none will result, and Democrats will retain their leadership in the issue. In these cases, no bill is passed even though both parties are interested in passing some form of legislation. This happened to Medicare in 1960 and the Family Assistance Plan in 1969, and could easily be the fate of health care legislation in the next few years.

Certain tactics are available to the Republicans to offset Democratic advantages. Often the Republicans do not in their hearts really want to go along with Democratic initiatives, but they fear that doing nothing will hurt them politically. If they can count on the Democrats to resist compromise, Republicans can make an offer that falls short of what the Democrats have bid without risk of its becoming law. This is good for the Republicans, who can show a general support for the idea of legislation but without having a law actually passed. Presumably, this at least partly diminishes the Democratic advantage. This stratagem carries with it a risk—that the Democrats will prove more flexible than expected and accept the Republican offer. Then the Republicans must either swallow bitter medicine and allow their proposal to become law, or back away from it.

For Democrats, the problem of the bidding-up strategy is that it often results in no legislation being passed, leaving Democratic constituencies worse off than they would have been if compromise legislation had passed. How can Democratic politicians help their constituents without either sacrificing political advantage or incurring the wrath of purists? Under divided party government, the solution to this dilemma is often to provoke a presidential veto, and then follow with legislation that the president will sign. By first passing legislation that satisfies the activists and enthusiasts among their followers, the Democrats show where their hearts really are. When the president vetoes this legislation, he underscores the difference between the two parties. Having tried to pass uncompromising legislation, an effort that staked out a position, the Democrats can then reach a compromise with the Republicans that allows legislation to pass. This appears to be what happened in 1989 in the case of minimum wage legislation. This course of action gets some benefits for constituents, but does tend to blur the differences between the parties. People who attend carefully to politics will understand the differences between Democrats and Republicans, but those whose attention is normally focused elsewhere may fail to see the difference, since the two parties do finally agree on legislation.

2   Strategies of Pursuit and Avoidance

Compromise gives each adversary
the satisfaction of thinking he has got
what he ought not to have, and is deprived
of nothing except what was justly his due.
—*Ambrose Bierce*

This chapter and the next two discuss a set of strategies that arise from competition between two parties or factions for political advantage on highly visible issues. One party begins with an advantage, meaning simply that it is the party most widely seen as likely to take vigorous action in the issue area. Democrats are advantaged in Social Security and health care, among other issues, because most people think they will fight hardest to protect and increase benefit levels. Republicans are advantaged on the crime and defense issues because people think they are tougher on criminals and stronger on defense. Generally speaking, at some point one party seizes upon an idea for social betterment and political advancement and uses it to solicit support from interested constituencies. At first, the other party ignores the issue and opposes action. Over time voters and interest groups come to see the issue as an important difference between the parties, and by this means the party that makes proposals and tries to get them passed becomes "advantaged" with these constituencies. Politicians who were initially against the proposal view the support it engenders with interest and alarm, and eventually become convinced that continued opposition will only hurt them. If the policy proposal is a wave approaching the beach, sure to be enacted, why not ride it in and get some of the credit rather than be crushed trying to stop it?

Efforts by a disadvantaged party to avoid political harm by changing its position in a dramatic way are not new, nor are they confined to the United States. Disraeli's astonishing proposal in 1867 to broaden suffrage in Great Britain far more than even the Liberals had suggested must count as one of the most famous and important instances of a party increasing its bid to escape a political disadvantage.[1] Although the analyses in this book are confined to the United States, the strategies are applicable in a wide array of circumstances.

Strategic disagreement can occur between parties or within them. The discussion here is for the most part in terms of interparty competition, but it applies equally to conflict between factions within a single party.

Efforts by a disadvantaged party to mitigate the harm an issue can do take several forms. In general, the disadvantaged party engages in tactics of "pursuit," meaning it offers a proposal that positions it closer than before to the advantaged party. The exact course chosen depends on the extent of the party's determination. If it is truly intent on reducing or eliminating the disadvantage, it may offer a proposal that matches or exceeds those offered by the advantaged party, and may be unwilling to allow the other party to outbid it. Determination on both sides to achieve ascendancy can produce a bidding war. If less determined, the disadvantaged party can offer a proposal that positions it near, but short of, the advantaged party. Depending on the response of the advantaged party, this can result either in the passage of a bill or in partisan bickering. If the disadvantaged party is equivocal about whether it is willing to do anything, but still worried about political damage, it might offer a modest proposal—but only if it is sure that the proposal will be rejected. This last possibility will be explored in the next chapter.

Avoiding an agreement that would bring about an improvement compared to the status quo is strategic *disagreement*. That is, these disagreements result not from the absence of a feasible agreement, but from tactics calculated to maintain political advantage. Politicians who engage in strategic disagreement do not strive to obtain the best possible deal that can be gotten at present for their constituents. When the disadvantaged party pursues its opponent out of fear it will suffer harm if it remains obdurate on the issue, it engages in strategic *agreement*. Party members may actively dislike the proposal they offer but recognize that political expediency requires them to hold their noses and get into the competition.

The importance of strategies of pursuit and avoidance derives from the prominence of the issues affected, not from the frequency with which the strategies are used, which is usually not very high. These strategies have played a part in some of the most significant legislative dramas of our time, having helped to delay substantially the enactment of both Medicare and federal aid to education, to kill welfare reform in 1969, and to block the enactment of Nixon's national health insurance proposal in 1974 and Carter's health care proposals in 1979 and 1980.[2] The American health care system would look far different today had ambitious politicians not rejected half a loaf when it was offered by Nixon and Carter. In other cases legislation passed, but it was distorted in unfortunate ways by competitive bidding between the parties. In the case of the Clean Air Act of 1970, competition between President Nixon and Senator Edmund Muskie, with helpful prodding from Ralph Nader, resulted in an auto emission standard that could not be met at the time and has not yet been attained.[3] A bidding war over Social Security benefits in 1972 between President Nixon, Representative Wilbur Mills, and Democratic senators led to a 20 percent increase in benefits.[4] In Ted Kennedy's unsuccessful effort to win the 1980 Democratic nomination away from President Carter, Kennedy strategically avoided agreement with Carter over comprehensive health insurance, and no bill was passed.[5] In the Bush administration, Democrats' refusals to compromise with Republicans doomed family-leave legislation and caused delays in the enactment of unemployment insurance.

Pursuit and avoidance occur only in conjunction with certain kinds of issues and under special circumstances. Highly visible issues that appeal to sizable constituencies whose votes are seen as movable from one party to another can readily stimulate competitive bidding between the parties. Since black voters are typically regarded as safely Democratic, pursuit and avoidance are unlikely to emerge in the consideration of civil rights legislation or other issues of particular concern to blacks. Because the elderly are much more likely to swing as a group from one party to the other, elderly issues are promising material for pursuit and avoidance tactics. Competition does not break out over issues with small audiences or over those that are remote from public consciousness. Only when two factions or parties seek to appeal to the same group do strategies of pursuit and avoidance emerge. When the parties seek support from different constituencies, rather than compete, they do their best to distance themselves from each other, producing stalemate, as discussed in chapter 5.

Few bills become the object of competitive bidding, partly because few are suitable. Most bills Congress considers deal with minor or technical issues and do not lend themselves to partisan politicking. Many issues fail to unite the Democratic members of Congress against Republicans, and thus are not useful for partisan purposes. In addition, a committee chairman who is not in the party mainstream might refuse to cooperate by reporting a confrontational bill. Or if the House of Representatives is inclined toward confrontational tactics, it can be frustrated by the unwillingness of the Senate to go along. After subtracting the bills that fail to excite the masses, and that do not unite one party against the other, we are left with a small residue of bills suitable for avoidance strategies. Even with these cases, it may be deemed more important to get a bill passed than to smite the president with an issue.

Calculations of the Disadvantaged Party

Faced with an issue that hurts them, parties, factions, or candidates may engage in strategic agreement, putting forward a plan or proposal they do not support, but which reduces their political disadvantage. Their goal may be to pass an ambitious bill and steal the issue from their opponent; to pass a modest bill to gain some credit, neutralize the issue, and keep a more extreme bill from passing; or merely to have a proposal on the table to shield them from criticism, and possibly to confuse the issue sufficiently so that no bill passes.

Despite its benefits, pursuit can be a perilous strategy, for it requires adopting a new and possibly dramatically different position on an issue. That can be unsettling to established relations within the party and between the party and some of its core constituencies. Constituencies that have been loyal to the disadvantaged party and that oppose taking action can be offended or alienated by the new position. Explaining to enthusiastic members of the party and its supporting constituencies why the party is taking a new position can be difficult. They may, after all, view concessions as betrayals of the correct party line. Some may refuse to believe that concessions are needed to forestall greater changes in the future.

A sensible goal of the disadvantaged party can be to offer a moderate proposal that passes and thus keeps more extreme legislation from passing in the future. This of course is exactly why supporters of extreme proposals dislike compromise. This strategy depends on unifying two groups: those who would prefer to pass no legislation but who nonetheless fear that inaction may lead to the enactment of an extreme bill; and those who favor passing a moderate bill, but who would vote for a more extreme bill in the absence of another viable alternative.

Luring hard-core opponents to vote for a bill they oppose, on the grounds that this may prevent a more extreme bill later, can be impossible. Many of those against change will oppose even minor reforms; unless they come to accept the inevitability of change they will oppose reformist efforts to hold the line against revolutionary change. And by the time the most stalwart resistance to reform has ended, the forces for change will be so powerful, and the moderates so few in number, that minor concessions by conservatives will be brushed aside. The same problem affects negotiations between governments and insurgent movements, as Stephen John Stedman writes:

> A common pattern in civil conflict is that at the beginning of civil wars, the insurgent movement makes demands that fall short of a complete political, social, and economic transformation. Governments . . . tend to avoid concessions and fight. At later stages of the fight, the government may believe that concessions are necessary, only to find that the demands of the insurgency have increased and what would have originally bought them a settlement is now rejected.[6]

Clean air legislation provides an example of how hard it can be to persuade archfoes of change to act strategically. Throughout nearly all of the 1980s, opponents of clean air legislation resisted passing any new legislation, knowing they had support from President Reagan. In 1988, the last year of the Reagan administration, Senator Robert Byrd, Democrat of West Virginia, and Representative John Dingell, Democrat of Michigan, both of whom had long been opponents of clean air legislation, became interested in passing legislation they had steadfastly opposed for seven years. They were convinced that the next president, regardless of party, would be more in favor of environmental legislation than Reagan, and that by passing a clean air bill in 1988 they could preclude the enactment of a stronger one later. Negotiations on the bill began but bogged down when utility companies, who probably should have favored this approach, refused to back the bill, thinking incorrectly that they would be able to hold off any bill even after the election.[7] Tom Tauke, a Republican representative from Iowa, said: "Most Washington representatives find it hard to explain to the CEO at their corporate headquarters why it was important to agree to limited changes now in order to avoid more sweeping changes later. That is short-sighted but it is the way business deals with Washington."[8]

Clean air proponents also understood that if they waited, they could get a better deal, and thus became less interested in a compromise than they would have been in 1984, for example. It might have been possible to pass a bill before the new president was elected, but the leaders of opposition forces were unable to convince vital allies (such as utility companies) that compromise was in fact necessary. So, just as the foot draggers became willing to make concessions, the enthusiasts of change lost interest in compromise. The very conditions that make one side more amenable to compromise make the other less.

In a similar case in the 1950s, the Eisenhower administration sought to pass limited legislation to make health insurance more widely available, only to see its efforts opposed by right-wing Republicans and the American Medical Association. Eisenhower saw the extremely modest health reinsurance bill drawn up by Secretary of HEW Oveta Culp Hobby as a way of holding the line against "socialized medicine" and was baffled and incensed by the shortsightedness of the AMA.[9] "How in the hell is the AMA going to stop socialized medicine if they oppose such bills as this? I don't think the American people are going to stand for being deprived of the opportunity to get medical insurance. If they don't get a bill like this, they will go for socialized medicine sooner or later and the AMA will have no one to blame but itself."[10] Leaders who want to act strategically can become extremely frustrated when the people who should be their allies cannot be persuaded to think strategically, or simply believe that they can hold out forever without making concessions.

Those with an extremely short time horizon may oppose all compromise and find themselves joined by those with a very long time horizon. The latter group can believe that in the long run, settling for a compromise that is "the best one can get" can be harmful in that it may obscure differences between the parties and thus prevent a battle on true principles in the future.[11] Conservatives could very well take the position that the Republican party should not allow itself to be tainted by any form of complicity in setting up New Deal–type programs—even if their participation could prevent the enactment of even worse programs—because any form of help in establishing the programs limits their ability to wage war against them in future elections. The goal of maintaining differences between the parties is flatly incompatible with strategic agreement.

Calculations of the Advantaged Party

When a Republican president proposes legislation that matches or comes close to the position supported by most Democrats, the Democrats face a classic political choice, typically expressed in the following form: "Do you want a bill or an issue?" If they accept the Republican offer, a bill can pass. In all likelihood, the Republican offer is less far-reaching or ambitious than most Democrats would prefer. The advantage of acquiescing is obvious: a bill will become law and its benefits realized quickly. The cost is slightly more subtle: the Democrats lose their political advantage over, and distinctiveness with respect to, the other party.

If they pass a bill close to what the president has requested, it will become law. The policy adopted will be an improvement over the status quo, and the welfare of the people who elected them will presumably be enhanced. The main disadvantage from the standpoint of Democratic representatives is that they sacrifice potential political advantage over the other party. If they agree to the bill the president proposes, the president can take as much credit for it as members of Congress can, and perhaps more. In addition, they will have gotten only half a loaf, and the enactment of this bill may preclude the passage of another, better bill in the near future.

Now let us suppose that they decide to go ahead and pass a bill closer to their true preference, despite the possibility that it will be vetoed. A number of advantages are associated with this option and often make it far preferable to agreeing to the president's proposal. First, the president may in fact sign the bill, preferring to avoid confrontation. Second, if the president does veto the bill, the Democrats have an issue for the next campaign. Their passage of the bill combined with the president's veto present very clearly the distinction between the two parties, which can be very useful for campaign purposes. Third, should the president veto the bill, there is the possibility of an override of the veto, which is the political equivalent of a grand slam in baseball. A successful override allows the Democrats to get their preferred bill passed and to take all the credit for doing so. It also shows the president in a bad light and splits his party.

Two significant disadvantages attend this more confrontational strategy. First, there is the strong possibility that no bill will be passed. Second, the public likes bipartisanship; a party that rejects compromise can develop the reputation of being excessively quarrelsome.

It is possible to explain what factors enter into the decision of whether to avoid an agreement, but the complexity of the choice probably makes it impossible to predict in advance what strategy will be employed in any given situation. The following list of issues indicates the nature of the calculation, but, as R. Douglas Arnold explained in a similar situation, "does not yield a unique outcome."[12]

An obviously important factor in determining whether one should strategically avoid agreement is the cost of waiting for another opportunity to pass the bill. In general, the lower the cost of delay and the shorter the delay, the more attractive disagreement will be and the less willing politicians will be to enter into compromise. The cost of delay is determined by a number of factors: when the next election is, how likely one's position is to be strengthened by the election, how dire the circumstances of one's constituents, and how likely constituents are to seek retribution should legislation not pass. If the next election or other opportunity for getting a better or equally good deal appears to be far in the future, the cost of employing a strategy of disagreement rises. Thus the advantaged party is more likely to agree to compromises immediately after an election than immediately before.

The closer the election, the more likely the advantaged party is to practice avoidance, both because it will want to protect the issue for the election, and because it can get a better bill later if the party does well in the election. We can consider this a function of a balancing between competing goals: helping constituents and winning elections. If the election is imminent, the Democrats can avoid agreement, hoping the issue will help them win the next election; they will also know that the failure of legislation need hurt constituents for only a relatively brief period. After their glorious victory in the election they can pass a better bill than was possible before. But when the next election is far off, the usefulness of confrontation declines. A battle fought three years before the elections may be scarcely remembered on election day. And without legislation now, constituents must suffer without any relief for a prolonged period.

The better the advantaged party expects to do in the election, the less inclined it will be to compromise. But even a party that does not expect to do well may want to avoid a compromise so that it can get some benefit from the issue. Then, after the election, it can accept a compromise. A disadvantaged party that expects to do badly in the upcoming election will be more likely to make a bold offer than one that expects to do well. After the election, the disadvantaged party will be less interested in offering a compromise. Paradoxically, after the election the advantaged party will be more likely to accept a compromise. The conditions that make one side more willing to compromise simultaneously make the other side less willing.

A failure to reach agreement that deprives voters of existing benefits will anger them more than a failure to provide new benefits, even though, in a perfectly rational calculus, the two are identical. Words can hardly describe the anger of constituents should their stream of government checks be disrupted by a political stalemate. But if the benefits lost are purely prospective, the constituents will hardly notice their deprivation and will raise much less ruckus—perhaps none. Benefits people have come to expect are valued more highly than prospective benefits.[13] Thus bargaining over the reauthorization of an existing program is less likely to generate avoidance tactics than legislation creating a new program.

The propensity to compromise will be influenced by the extent to which parties and politicians feel a need to produce tangible results. Confrontational strategies often do not lead to the passage of legislation and may promote a perception that the government squabbles a lot but does nothing. If constituents are in an angry mood, wanting action, not symbolism, they may punish politicians who do not deliver the goods. This would naturally increase the cost of delay and make disagreement less desirable.

If proponents of a new law believe that public sentiment will be more in their favor next year than at present, and that the next election will return a government more favorable to their bill than the current government, the cost of delay is very small and they will be disinclined to compromise. The legislation possible today will be moderate in scope. A better strategy may be to press the issue in order to publicize it, but to accept no compromise. In the early 1970s the public was clearly becoming more interested in environmentalism, and thus the advocates of environmental legislation were in no mood to compromise, believing that if they could not pass the bill they wanted now, they would be able to after the next election.

Issues that unify one party against another are ideal for strategies of disagreement, particularly under divided party government. The more a party is unified on an issue, the more likely it is to use strategies of disagreement. To embarrass the president by forcing him to veto a popular bill, Congress must first pass it; and in highly partisan issue areas a great deal of party unity is required to pass the bill. Many issues divide the parties and consequently offer no partisan advantages. Immigration legislation in the 1980s was a potentially inflammatory issue that was resolved without resorting to political gamesmanship. Both parties had significant groups who would have been very happy to demagogue the issue, criticizing the other party for opening up the gates to foreign elements and throwing Americans out of jobs. But both parties also had large constituencies that were very interested in providing for relatively easy access of Mexican labor to the United States. The inability of either party to launch an effective political attack helped immigration legislation immeasurably.

Issues removed from the immediate concerns of voters are more likely to be resolved in quiet, nonpublic, cooperative negotiations. Cable television regulation concerns millions of voters, but few become exercised over the issue, and negotiations about it are conducted mostly in private, between the parties most actively concerned: the cable industry and its direct competitors. Highly salient issues, such as taxes and Social Security benefits, lend themselves much more readily to manipulation. A politician knows there will be an audience because no one needs to be convinced that these are important issues.

When there is active competition for a party's presidential nomination, candidates for the nomination may be reluctant to accept a compromise out of fear of alienating a constituency whose support they need.[14] When the party nomination is assured for one candidate, intraparty competition will be dampened, but when the out party has several candidates positioning themselves for a nomination battle, they may choose to compete by outbidding one another. Similarly, if a sitting president appears vulnerable, contenders within his own party may seek to undermine his leadership by making grand promises to constituency groups.

The orientation of leaders toward conflict can also be important, though difficult to understand in any systematic way. Some people by nature seem more inclined to generate conflict. Speaker Jim Wright, for instance, believed in confrontation.[15] His immediate successor, Tom Foley, was far more inclined toward accommodation, and was criticized for that. Both speakers dealt with the same issues and with the same people, so it would be hard to call upon changed circumstances to account for the different styles of Wright and Foley. Little changed except the person of the speaker, yet there was a significant shift in behavior. Personality, style, and personal preference are the only reasonable explanations.

Bargaining Advantage

The nature and structure of party coalitions limit what a party can agree to, and as a result, some issues naturally favor one party. In Social Security politics, for example, the Democrats can normally bid higher than the Republicans. In the contemporary politics of tax cutting, the Republicans can cut lower than the Democrats.[16] The asymmetrical relationship of the parties to constituencies creates opportunities and incentives for competitive bidding over policy, and also constitutes an important restriction on bidding wars. If both parties were equally capable of attracting the support of all constituencies, neither party could ever outbid the other, and the enterprise would seem useless.

Each of the parties has a collection of issues it promotes and constituencies it seeks to appeal to. Both parties have core constituencies, composed of groups of voters and supporters they can count on to a large extent, and more peripheral constituencies, which are those whose votes and support they would like, but cannot rely upon. The parties must maintain their core support. Consequently, in their efforts to gain additional support among peripheral constituencies, they cannot normally embrace policy positions antithetical to those of their core constituencies.

The nature of existing party coalitions seriously constrains policy bidding because politicians and parties must maintain some level of consistency. This would not be a problem if politicians could offer all things to all people—but they cannot. One cannot promise Medicare to the old and the maintenance of the existing health care system to doctors; one cannot promise both adherence to the minimalist state and new government initiatives. As much as some contemporary Democrats would like to shake the "tax and spend" label, they cannot promise to cut taxes and spending as much as the Republicans. Doing so would undercut their ability to fulfill other, more important Democratic promises. Republicans would like to lose their reputation as less friendly to Social Security than Democrats, but their core identity as a party of low taxes makes it virtually impossible to compete with Democrats on this issue.

The Republican advantage on tax reduction stems from the fact that Republicans are generally less interested than Democrats in having the government do things that cost money. They can advocate tax reductions without foreclosing the possibility of achieving their other goals. Tax cuts keep Democrats from doing other things they would like to, and thus they will seldom be able to outbid Republicans in tax fights. Republicans can outbid Democrats on defense spending for the same reason. When Republicans allocate large amounts of money to defense, they take it from domestic programs that they do not support strongly. For Democrats to match a Republican defense bid means starving other, higher priorities.

A key element of political strategy is for a party to discover issues that are popular with swing voters that do not alienate their core constituencies, but do offend the other party's core constituencies, or which at least split the other party. Such issues give one party a clear-cut advantage.

The balance of this chapter explores in detail several instances of pursuit and avoidance and two different routes it can take. The first is the failure of legislation to pass due to the avoidance of one party.

I examine three instances of pursuit and avoidance in the area of health insurance, in each of which there appears to have been a real chance of reaching agreement had enthusiasts among Democrats responded favorably to compromise proposals. However, in all these instances no legislation passed.

The specific empirical claim advanced here is that delays in enacting Medicare and other forms of national health insurance have been due in substantial part to strategic disagreement. The alternative explanation I seek to discredit is that the participants in these negotiations were so far apart that no agreement was possible. Serious, moderate reforms were put forward, and if adopted would have improved on the status quo, but the most enthusiastic supporters of change would not accept less than all that they wanted. Had Democrats been more willing to compromise, Medicare could have been adopted in 1960, and national health insurance in 1974. Had Senator Edward Kennedy not been involved in a fight with Jimmy Carter for the Democratic presidential nomination, he might have supported Carter's health care proposals and helped them pass.

The second route considered here is a bidding war, which occurs when the pursuing party is unwilling to be outdone. To illustrate bidding wars, I examine the politics of Social Security benefit increases under Richard Nixon, especially in 1972, when Congress passed and Nixon signed a 20 percent increase in benefits.

Strategic Disagreement in Health Care, 1960–1978

Medicare in 1960

Medicare legislation failed to be adopted in 1960 because Democrats in the Senate could not procure enough votes to pass their plan, and because they were unwilling to settle for the alternative proposal put forward by Republicans. The tale of Medicare in 1960 is complex, involving bargaining within the Republican party as well as between Democrats and Republicans. Ultimately, however, modest

Republican proposals were not passed for lack of Democratic support.

The idea of government-funded health care for the elderly was not new, but Republican support for it was.[17] President Truman had proposed such legislation, but it was probably premature and was soundly defeated. By 1960, Democrats in the House and Senate had been agitating across the country for several years to generate support for a system of health care for the elderly based on the principle of social insurance (i.e., a contributory system, like Social Security), and had made significant progress in developing a following, particularly among the elderly.[18] The most prominent exponent of such legislation was Representative Aime Forand, Democrat of Rhode Island, the fourth-ranking Democrat on the House Ways and Means Committee. Beginning in 1957, he annually introduced legislation to create a Social Security–based health care system for the aged. The AFL-CIO Department of Social Security wrote the bill, which provided for protection for surgery, sixty days of hospitalization, and sixty days of home nursing care, all funded by an increase in the payroll tax.[19] First they asked Wilbur Mills, chairman of Ways and Means, to introduce the bill, and when he declined they moved down the list of Democrats on the committee until they got to Forand. Forand worried that sponsoring the legislation would get him in trouble with constituents, since the proposal could be likened to that perennial bugbear, socialized medicine. But Nelson Cruikshank, who headed the Social Security department at the AFL-CIO, assured Forand that introducing the bill would cause no problems. With some reluctance, Forand agreed.[20] Far from causing trouble, his association with the Medicare idea made him a national hero among the elderly. Each year the issue gained in prominence and by 1960 had become the most important issue of the year in Congress and one of the biggest issues in the presidential campaign. Meanwhile the AMA, adamantly opposed to any such nonsense, geared up its lobbying apparatus to defeat the monstrosity.

Gradually, the Eisenhower administration changed its position on the issue. Previously, President Eisenhower had declared that medical insurance was a matter for private, not public, action. The administration's goal was to work to encourage insurance companies to offer health insurance to the aged, and its official position was that private industry could take care of the problem. By 1959, after the Department of HEW conducted a study into the extent of the problem, the administration ceased to argue that private insurance by itself could be adequate. But it made no recommendation.

In late 1959 the president changed his mind to support the idea of health insurance. There followed a protracted battle within the administration to produce a plan that would be acceptable to the Republican party. The precipitating event was a meeting in October 1959 of Eisenhower with Robert P. Burroughs, an insurance and pension expert concerned about health care for the elderly. He argued that the elderly could not afford premiums on private health insurance because expenses went up as their ability to pay declined. He urged a social insurance approach, whereby people would pay for their health care in retirement by means of a payroll tax during their working years. Burroughs went on to claim that "compulsory coverage for this purpose, which is the only way the problem will be solved, presents no issues, philosophical or political, that have not already arisen and been dealt with acceptably in the social security system as it is now constituted."[21] Eisenhower sent Burroughs over to meet with Secretary Flemming, who was pleasantly surprised to learn that the president now appeared to favor the social insurance approach. In a meeting a week later with Flemming, Eisenhower indicated support for the idea of a compulsory plan based on a payroll deduction. Eisenhower was particularly interested in creating a system to take care of catastrophic expenses, suggesting a $250 deductible. Eisenhower seemed keenly aware of the political issues involved; according to a memorandum of the meeting, "the President said with regard to Mr. Burrough's suggestion that the opposition will be making proposals of this kind and seeking credit for it. If something like this is to be done, he would like to have the Administration get some credit."[22] The department of HEW began to develop legislation to implement the new directive. In separate press conferences in February, 1960, Eisenhower and Flemming discussed the developing plans; both indicated that the ultimate legislative proposal would involve an increase in the payroll tax of one-fourth of 1 percent.[23]

After Eisenhower's initial endorsement of social insurance, there followed a series of tactical retreats, primarily for the purpose of maintaining some measure of unity among Republicans. In March Eisenhower retreated on the social insurance issue. He still wanted a bill, but not one based on Social Security. Evidently the AMA had a most effective lobbyist—Eisenhower's personal physician—who reminded the president of a campaign pledge not to support a social insurance approach to health care, and this persuaded him to back away from reliance on Social Security.[24] HEW went on to produce a voluntary health care plan for the elderly and persuaded the president and vice president to back it. Then this plan too was rejected in mid-March after a meeting with legislative leaders,[25] sending Flemming back to the drawing board. These abrupt changes were evidence of a tremendous tussle among Republicans, as the president sought to devise a plan that would compete seriously with the Forand approach without irretrievably alienating the core of the party. Although Eisenhower and Flemming agreed that a social insurance approach to health care involved no question of principle not previously addressed in Social Security, this view was not generally accepted within the Republican party. Many in the party disputed even the need for medical assistance for the elderly. The main criterion a plan had to satisfy to avoid Republican opposition was that it not be "compulsory." If the plan were not compulsory, it would not be "socialized medicine."[26]

However much some Republicans might have wanted to kill the

entire idea, that was generally regarded as infeasible, for it would have given the entire issue to the Democrats. Moreover, there was a real danger that the Forand bill or some variation of it would pass. Having a credible Republican bill would help block passage of a Democratic bill by halting the erosion of Republican unity. Liberal Republicans who faced constituency pressure on the health care issue would feel compelled to show their support for the idea by voting for a Democratic bill, if only a Democratic bill were available. Republican support might thus push Democratic legislation over the top, and thus present the president with the difficult choice of accepting a bill he did not like, or vetoing it and handing the Democrats a golden issue. Thus it was imperative that the administration have a bill at least, which could, in the words of Senator Saltonstall, "be a rallying point for Republicans in opposing the other proposals." Eisenhower noted the importance of Republicans in Congress having something they could vote for: "Certainly Horatius at the bridge did not have to stand there empty handed." Vice President Richard Nixon "spoke of the necessity for a choice of the lesser evil since it seemed apparent that the Forand bill or some substitute would be approved."[27] Nixon was said by the *New York Times* to believe "that the party cannot afford to take a negative position on what has become a pressing social problem with major political implications."[28] Nixon was at that time the all but inevitable Republican nominee for the presidency, and he could not have relished the prospect of running for president with the Republican party officially against any kind of medical assistance for the old. It was clearly in his interest to induce the administration to make at least a token gesture on behalf of medical care in order to blunt the Democratic advantage.[29]

While Flemming sought the magic formula that would not alienate Republican conservatives, Republican liberals began to act on their own. Senator Jacob Javits of New York drafted his own plan, which he intended to introduce in the Senate. The advantage in restraining Javits was that the administration's bill, when it emerged, would be better calculated to unite all Republicans. Javits, a liberal, would be less concerned than the administration to produce a bill that conservative Republicans could support.[30] Ultimately Javits did introduce his bill. It was not given a hearing by the Senate Finance Committee, but he introduced it as a floor amendment.

On May 2 Flemming got a "reluctant green light" from the president for his oft-rewritten health plan, and presented it to Congress on May 4.[31] It was called Medicare, the first use of this term, and it was both more conservative and more liberal than the Forand bill. We can compare proposals on three separate dimensions: services covered, population covered, and financing. The administration's proposal covered a far wider range of medical services than anything offered up to that time by the Democrats. It would cover up to 180 days of hospital care, unlimited nursing care, surgical benefits, and nearly all other medical expenses. The Forand bill, by contrast, covered a more limited range of hospital and nursing care, and no other expenses. The entire population over sixty-five was eligible for coverage under the administration's plan, though they would have to enroll by paying an annual fee of $24. The Forand proposal provided coverage only for Social Security recipients, leaving out some 4.2 million people over sixty-five who were not under the Social Security umbrella. The administration's proposal was funded partly by enrollment contributions, but primarily by appropriations from both federal and state governments. An additional important feature of the plan was the inclusion of a very substantial deductible of $250 for individuals and $400 for couples; it also required a 20 percent co-payment.[32] The Forand bill had no deductible and required neither an enrollment fee nor a co-payment. Funding would come exclusively from a Social Security–based payroll tax.

Comparing the plans is complex because the two approaches have somewhat offsetting advantages and disadvantages. The Forand bill covered a limited range of medical services, but it made up for this deficiency to some extent by having neither deductible nor co-payment requirements. The administration's plan covered an admirably wide range of services, but the large deductible and 20 percent co-payment would still leave many people in financial distress. Neither plan seems straightforwardly superior. The other crucial issue, on which there was a clear difference, concerned funding. The For-and bill lay clearly within the social insurance tradition characterized by an earmarked tax with mandatory participation, while Flemming's plan relied on appropriations from both state and federal governments.

There were distinct differences between the two plans, but these differences might seem to the naive observer to be less important than the magnitude of the concession just made by the Republicans, and it is hard to believe that the remaining differences explain the near complete hostility with which Democrats greeted the administration's concessions. The GOP had never before agreed on the need for federal action on the senior health care issue, but in 1960 it came forward with a plan that actually exceeded in some respects the coverage of the Democratic plans and that was much closer to the Democratic position than to the status quo. One might easily imagine that these circumstances would have seemed to favor some kind of negotiated agreement. But when the Flemming proposal emerged, it met an unremittingly hostile reaction, not just from conservatives, which was to be expected, but also from liberals. Flemming appeared before the House Ways and Means Committee and the Senate Finance Committee to explain his plan. Neither committee gave him an encouraging reception.

Conservatives considered the plan nothing but an opening wedge for socialized medicine. The AMA said the bill was based on the "false premise that almost all persons over 65 need health care and cannot afford it. That is not a fact."[33] Senator Barry Goldwater, Republican of Arizona, called it "socialized medicine" and "part of a dime store New Deal." Wilbur Mills, whose support in his capacity of chair of the House Ways and Means Committee was vital, made no public comment on the bill, but his reaction was reported to be "clearly unfavorable."[34]

The plan was not completely abandoned by conservatives. Charles Halleck had been consulted extensively by the administration in formulating the plan, and he stood by it after its announcement, even though he privately believed there was no need for such a program and had consistently opposed it in meetings with Eisenhower. He praised the plan as "the answer to one of today's pressing problems,"[35] and sent a note congratulating Flemming on his testimony before the Ways and Means Committee. But even if the Flemming plan had no chance of adoption, it could be politically beneficial to Republicans: "Privately some Republicans said the Administration had provided political solace for the party's legislators if nothing else. Support of the 'Medicare' plan, they explained, will at least help shield themselves against the heavy political pressures generated by the health-insurance issue."[36]

Secretary Flemming testified in executive session before the House Ways and Means Committee, which at the time was considering Social Security legislation, to which health care legislation could be appended. By a vote of seventeen to eight, the committee had already rejected the idea of increasing the Social Security tax to finance health care, which ruled out the Forand bill. Ultimately, the Ways and Means Committee reached an impasse on the competing plans, dividing into three factions, none of which could command a majority. There were the Democrats who favored the Forand bill, the Republicans who favored the Flemming approach, and finally, a group of Democrats and Republicans opposed to both Flemming's and Forand's approaches.

Conservative opposition was to be expected. The lack of conservative support meant that if the plan was to find a majority in Congress, that majority would be composed of moderates and liberals. But liberals offered a more uniformly negative reception to the Flemming plan than did the conservatives. A Ways and Means Democrat called the Flemming plan a "Townsend Plan–Rube Goldberg scheme."[37] The AFL-CIO, a leading Democratic constituent, was utterly hostile, opposing the adoption of any health care scheme not based on Social Security. George Meany, its president, called the administration's proposal "worse than no bill at all." The executive council of the AFL-CIO claimed the proposal had been offered to "meet the demands of an election year rather than the urgent needs of the aged."[38] Newspaper accounts of the time include no reports of any Democrats offering any support for the Flemming proposal.

The liberal response deserves careful analysis. This was the closest the two parties had ever been on the subject of health care for the elderly. Why, when the administration had just conceded a great deal of ground, did Democrats in Congress not offer even a little bit of encouragement? Why did liberals not consider this an opportunity for initiating serious discussions rather than an occasion for criticizing the administration? The answer, I believe, stems from the nature of political competition between the two parties. The Democrats had the upper hand on the issue, due to their earlier sponsorship and support of the Forand bill. For them to come to an agreement with the Republicans now, on the eve of the 1960 presidential election, would have sacrificed that advantage. This they were not willing to do. Second, if a voluntary program of health care were to be adopted, a program based on social insurance might have been impossible to adopt later on. With fewer people in need, the constituency for further changes would have been reduced.

Passing a bill required compromise; of this there could be little question. When Senator Vance Hartke, Democrat of Indiana, criticized Flemming's plan for not being based on Social Security, Flemming based his defense on political expediency, observing that the Ways and Means Committee had voted on the Forand bill and defeated it seventeen to eight. He pointed out that "the possibility of using the Social Security approach has been under discussion for a period of ten years" and that "if we really want to make progress in dealing with the needs of our fellow human beings, we should recognize as a fact that we are having trouble getting off the ground by using the Social Security approach" and consider other alternatives, such as the state-federal approach advocated by the Eisenhower administration. This was a classic appeal for political pragmatism; Hartke's response was to imply that Flemming had called the Social Security approach un-American.[39]

Democratic opposition to a Medicare plan not based on Social Security was due in part to the fact that the AFL-CIO, one of the Democrats' main constituency groups, was dead set against any other financing arrangement. In addition, Democrats knew they had an excellent election year issue, and were not inclined to trade away that advantage for a compromise Medicare bill. Senator John Kennedy, then a presidential candidate, spoke on the issue repeatedly, denouncing the administration for its lack of concern on the issue. By not acceding to the Republican plan, the issue remained alive and he could emphasize the differences between Democrats and Republicans. As soon as the two sides agreed on a bill, the difference between them would disappear, and with it any political advantage.

The administration's plan posed a challenge to the Democrats since it outbid the Forand bill in important respects, particularly in providing assistance to all the elderly, including those not on Social Security. The Democratic response was to increase the bid. On the day following the official unveiling of the administration's plan, Senator Pat McNamara, Democrat of Michigan, introduced legislation to compensate for inadequacies in the Forand plan. McNamara had sixteen cosponsors, including the three main contenders for the Democratic presidential nomination.[40] Having been matched in their bid by the Republicans, with the McNamara amendment Democrats raised their bid accordingly.[41]

With all the bids on the table, the House Ways and Means Committee set to work. Ways and Means was more conservative than the House as a whole, so when Aime Forand offered his bill as an amendment, it was defeated by a substantial margin. The committee then went on to append to the Social Security bill a minimal medical plan that provided assistance only to aged indigents. The total cost of the program was about one-third of the cost of either the Flemming or Forand plans. This passed on the House floor as part of a general Social Security bill, protected from amendments by a closed rule. Many observers believed that if the whole House had had the chance to vote on the Forand bill, it would have passed it.

The House bill then went to the Senate Finance Committee, where much of the same action was repeated. Senator Clinton Anderson, Democrat of New Mexico, offered a form of the Forand bill as an amendment to the committee bill, and intended to offer it again on the floor if necessary. The committee, dominated by conservatives of both parties, gave the Anderson and Flemming plans short shrift and went on to report out a medical program that was similar to that written in Ways and Means, targeted exclusively at the poor among the aged. The right of unlimited debate and amendment in the Senate meant that the actions of the committee did not preclude consideration of alternatives by the full chamber.

The Democratic strategy was to pass the Anderson amendment in the Senate, force the House to go along, and present the bill to the president. Regardless of whether Eisenhower vetoed the bill, the Democrats would come out winners. If he signed the bill, then they got legislation they wanted and could boast of having forced the president to go along with them. If he vetoed the bill, they would be left with an excellent issue for the fall campaign. Best of all would be a veto followed by an override. The immense value of a veto to the Democrats was clearly recognized at the time. William Schnitzler of the AFL-CIO said, "this Administration may be able to threaten a veto; it may be able to corral the 'one third and one' necessary to sustain a veto, but if it does that, it faces political suicide in the coming elections." Referring to Nixon he said: "No Presidential candidate, saddled with such a veto, can hope to be elected next November."[42] Campaigning in California for the Democratic nomination, Stuart Symington said that medical care for the aged was a key issue in the campaign. He expected that if Congress passed the bill, the president would veto it, and that would veto "Nixon right out of the White House."[43] One might easily imagine that the Democrats preferred a veto to enactment of any of the bills then before Congress. It was reported that liberal Democrats in the Senate actually sought a far more expansive medical program than called for in any of the pending bills, and thus were not as interested in passing a bill in 1960 as in making use of the issue.[44] Both sides were intensely concerned with the disposition of political credit. "The Democrats in control of Congress," a *New York Times* editorial explained, "have not too much interest in producing legislation for which the Republican Administration might take credit—and vice versa."[45]

Ultimately, Republican strategy was successful. Eisenhower's twin goals throughout this episode were to help out elderly people with health care expenses and to reduce or eliminate Democratic political advantages in the health care issue. It is clear from his comments in cabinet and legislative leaders' meetings that both purposes were on Eisenhower's mind. As events proceeded it became evident that his fellow Republicans agreed it was important to neutralize Democratic advantages, but they did not believe legislation was necessary and offered little support for the goal of actually passing legislation. The administration's effort increasingly served the purpose of damage control. In one view, then, the legislation proposed by Flemming and Javits was an honest effort to do something good for senior citizens—and that is certainly what Flemming and Javits themselves intended. For much of the rest of the Republican party, however, the real purpose of this legislation was not to become law, but to siphon support from Forand-type legislation. There would be some danger that Democrats would accept a Republican proposal, in which case decoy legislation could be unintentionally enacted; but in the politically charged atmosphere of the summer of 1960 there was little danger that Democrats would accept a health plan not based on Social Security. Confident of Democratic intransigence, Republicans such as Halleck who wanted no legislation to pass could sanctimoniously charge that the Democrats wanted an issue, not a bill, when of course Halleck wanted both the bill and the issue to disappear.

The main Republican goal was to keep a bill that Eisenhower could not sign from reaching his desk, because a veto of a health care bill on the eve of the election would be politically damaging. The Javits amendment, which replaced the Flemming proposal as the focus of Republican efforts, did serve as a point around which Republicans could rally, and gave hesitating Republicans an excuse not to vote for Democratic amendments. If Republicans had argued against Democratic legislation without offering an alternative of their own, they would have been taking a position against the idea of health care assistance for the aged. Even if that was their position, it was best to avoid enunciating it at a time when the public was aroused on the issue. The presence of an administration alternative allowed Republicans to take the much safer position of agreeing with the Democrats' goal, opposing only the means employed. Republicans feeling pressure from constituents may have felt compelled to support some form of health legislation. The Republican alternative allowed them to show support without any danger of enacting a bill. The strategy worked. At each stage in the process—in the House Ways and Means Committee, the Senate Finance Committee, and finally on the Senate floor—Republicans consistently voted for Republican alternatives and against Forand-like proposals. As the Anderson amendment went down to defeat, Kennedy said that if Congress could not pass the Democratic plan, "I favor desisting here and taking the issue to the people." He did not want to "pass bills that are hopelessly inadequate. I don't think that would serve any purpose."[46]

Since Democrats would not support Republican proposals and vice versa, only the minimal Kerr-Mills legislation passed. This result was probably the best Nixon could hope for. Emphasizing differences between the parties on the Medicare issue would benefit Kennedy, while minimizing them would benefit Nixon. Nixon and Kennedy both supported more legislation to implement fairly comprehensive health coverage for the aged, though they disagreed on the means. Nixon and Kennedy both supported Kerr-Mills, and when it was passed, both Nixon and Kennedy asserted that Kerr-Mills was totally inadequate. Of course there were important differences between the candidates, but the failure of the Democrats to force Eisenhower to veto a bill muddied the waters. Nixon could, and did, campaign by calling Kerr-Mills "most inadequate," and asserting that "the next Congress should deal with revision of the program at the earliest opportunity."[47] That was also the position of the Kennedy campaign.

The result of the Medicare battle of 1960 was not very satisfying for Kennedy, but it may have been better than passing a compromise bill. Provoking an Eisenhower veto of a health care bill would have been the best result for Kennedy, showing the Republicans to be hard-hearted toward the elderly. But a compromise agreement between Democrats and Republicans would have obliterated any difference between the parties and undermined any credibility of Kennedy in attacking Republicans on the health care issue. Worst of all, adopting a voluntary, state-federal health plan in 1960 might have precluded adopting a more expansive Medicare plan in the future.

Apart from passing a health bill, which some Republicans genuinely sought to do, the Republican strategy was to minimize Democratic political advantages stemming from the health issue. From the administration's standpoint, the best result would have been the passage of the Flemming plan or something like it. The worst would be the enactment of the Forand bill; since the administration had lobbied very actively against it, its passage would have presented the president with the unpleasant decision of whether to veto it. Regardless of how he decided, he would lose. The second-best alternative was the enactment of neither plan—and offering the Flemming plan could very well have been calculated to keep any bill from passing. Liberal Republicans wanted to be able to vote for some kind of significant health bill. Without an administration plan to vote for, some would almost certainly have voted for the Anderson amendment— possibly enough of them to pass it.

When the bill came to the Senate floor, there was no evidence of compromise on any side and party lines held firmly. Richard Nixon was on the Senate floor, rounding up votes and acting as a party whip. In voting on the Anderson amendment, only one Republican joined forty-three Democrats in support. Nineteen Democrats, all from southern or border states, voted against it, sending the Anderson amendment to defeat. Jacob Javits offered the principal amendment for the Republicans, a modified version of the Flemming plan. All but five Republicans voted for it, while no Democrats did, and so it too died.[48] All the amending activity left the original committee provisions undisturbed. This was a strange result, in that Congress passed a health bill that both Democrats and Republicans agreed was inadequate.

The Javits and Anderson amendments were not far apart, and they were certainly closer to each other than they were to the program that actually became law. Both broke new ground in calling for a major federal role in providing health care for large numbers of the elderly, and between them they commanded the support of sixty-seven senators. Understandable though it may be in the logic of competitive party politics, it is still somewhat perverse that they could not overcome the issues that divided them and enact a significant health bill. That would take another five years, until liberal Democratic strength in Congress had increased substantially and the composition of the tax committees changed.

Evidence suggests there was a real opportunity to pass a medical care bill in 1960. Eisenhower and Flemming seem to have been genuinely interested in passing a bill. A handful of liberal Republicans wanted a bill. Democrats wanted a medical care program. With a Republican president prodding some reluctant Republican members to join with liberal Democrats, a program could have been enacted. This was, moreover, the only way that a bill could pass. Democrats alone could not generate a majority because of defections among the southern wing of the party; consequently a coalition of Democrats and Republicans was required. Given this necessity, having a Republican president sympathetic to the cause was highly advantageous. The vast majority of Republicans had a deep antipathy to any kind of "socialized medicine" and would not vote for it. But with Eisenhower pushing them to vote for his plan, some undoubtedly would have, and even did, in 1960.

Waiting a year until Kennedy was elected president (if one cared to accept that gamble) would not help pass a medical care bill. The greatest problem was getting the bill out of Congress, not avoiding a presidential veto. Unless Kennedy were elected with huge new majorities in Congress (which he was not), getting the bill out of Congress would, oddly enough, be harder than with a Republican in the White House. Eisenhower could help by prodding Republicans to support a moderate bill. With a Democrat in the White House, only a handful of Republicans in Congress would support any major health bill. Conservative Democrats would vote against the bill regardless of who was President.[49] Kennedy was elected president in 1960. Democrats picked up no new seats in the Senate, while losing twenty-one seats in the House. Not passing the Republican health care proposals may have helped Kennedy win the election, but it did nothing in the way of passing health care legislation, which was not passed until 1965, at which point the Democrats had massive majorities in both chambers of Congress, and had little need to bargain with Republicans.

Even in 1965, when Medicare was passed, pursuit strategies continued to have a strong influence on Medicare politics. Avoidance disappeared as a Democratic tactic since this was the high-water mark of Democratic strength in Congress, a time to pass legislation, not jockey for future advantage. Republicans' efforts to establish their credentials as serious players in health care policy making contributed to making the bill substantially more ambitious than it would have been had Republicans stayed out of the bidding.

The 1964 elections returned the most Democratic Congress since the 1930s, and it was seen as inevitable that Medicare would pass in that Congress. According to Theodore Marmor, "The only question remaining was the precise form health insurance legislation would take."[50] Kennedy administration proposals on health care had fared badly in Congress from 1961 through 1964, both because the Ways and Means Committee was unwilling to let the bills come to the floor, and because there may have been a shortage of votes on the floor (although Ways and Means never allowed for confirmation of this suspicion). Acting cautiously now that success seemed possible, the administration retained its proposals from previous years, which were somewhat scaled-back versions of the Forand plan. Because it did not cover physicians' services or surgical costs, the administration's plan was widely criticized for its inadequacy.

Republicans had lost badly in the 1964 elections, and their losses were partially attributed to the stridency of Republican opposition to Medicare. To keep the Democrats from getting all credit for Medicare and to distance Republicans from the AMA, Representative John Byrnes, the senior Republican on Ways and Means, developed an alternative plan that covered a broader array of services and that was voluntary and financed by general revenues.[51]

It is impossible to know whether the Byrnes plan was intended to pass or merely to siphon off support from the administration's bill, but its effect was to cause the passage of a broader bill than the administration or the Ways and Means Committee Democrats had originally thought possible. Chairman Wilbur Mills surprised partisans from both sides by proposing a marriage of the Democratic plan for hospitalization insurance funded through Social Security to the

Republican plan for voluntary medical insurance.[52] Fear of Republican attacks had made the Democrats keep their plans modest, but the expansive benefits promised by Byrnes freed Democrats to propose a more ambitious Medicare plan.[53] There was no point in the Democrats' continuing to distinguish themselves from Republicans, since it was unlikely that conditions for passing a health insurance bill would improve in the future, and, as a result, they were not likely to engage in further bidding-up strategies.

Nixon and National Health Insurance in 1974

Early in 1974, caught in the turmoil of Watergate, President Richard Nixon declared the enactment of national health insurance his top domestic priority. His secretary of HEW, Caspar Weinberger, said: "Nothing should deter us from adding, this year, comprehensive health insurance protection to the basic security guarantees that America offers."[54] It is discouraging to reflect from our current vantage point that an opportunity to pass national health insurance presented itself in 1974—at a time when health care was far less expensive and reform would have been easier to manage—but was allowed to slip away.

The events of 1974 bear a striking resemblance to 1960. A Republican president proposed legislation that brought Republicans far closer to the Democrats than they had ever been. Democrats did not embrace the proposal, but instead held out for more at a later date, anticipating that the approaching elections would leave them with larger congressional majorities. Elections delivered the expected surge in Democratic seats, but increasing budget problems closed the window of opportunity for adopting expensive new government initiatives. As in 1960, the Republican offer represented a significant improvement over existing policy from the Democratic standpoint, and from the perspective of Democratic constituents, even if it was not ideal.

In February 1974 Nixon introduced his plan for national health insurance, and called for prompt congressional action. Nixon's proposal would have required all employers to offer health insurance to their employees, the employer paying 75 percent of the cost and the employee the rest. Employees would not be required to participate. Participants would pay a $450 deductible before payments would begin, and would be responsible for a 25 percent co-payment. But after a family had spent $1500 out of pocket, all subsequent expenses would be covered. The federal government would provide similar benefits to the poor under a revised Medicare program.

The chief Democratic rival was a plan sponsored by Senator Ted Kennedy and Representatives Martha Griffith (D-Mich.) and James Corman (D-Calif.), which would have provided comprehensive benefits without any co-payment or deductible. Participation would be mandatory, and the plan would be funded by a payroll tax.

Prospects for legislative action looked bright initially because two key players, Senator Ted Kennedy and Representative Wilbur Mills, appeared willing to abandon the standard Democratic plan and compromise. They introduced a joint proposal that paralleled Nixon's in important ways, but also had important differences. Under the Kennedy-Mills plan, participation would be mandatory and financing would be through a 4 percent payroll tax. The deductible was $300 and the co-payment 25 percent. After a family had paid $1,000 all subsequent expenses would be covered. In both plans lower-income individuals would pay smaller deductibles and co-payments.

The spirit of compromise shown by Kennedy and Mills was not shared by traditional Democratic constituencies. Organized labor, the Council of Senior Citizens, and consumer groups preferred the Griffiths-Corman bill. Supporters of Griffiths-Corman urged waiting until after the elections, which it was hoped would produce "veto-proof" Democratic majorities in Congress and allow passage of a health care bill without compromise. Weinberger criticized this approach: "We firmly reject the views of those few who counsel that no action be taken until some vague future time when they believe that the plan they personally favor could be enacted without change."[55]

The legislation stalled in the face of partisan squabbling and the prospects of a protracted Nixon impeachment. But even after Nixon's resignation, Ford still backed the idea of passing a health bill in 1974. Ford's enthusiasm may have been due in some measure to the inevitability of huge Democratic gains in the 1974 congressional elections. As organized labor grew more confident and willing to wait, the medical establishment got worried and became more inclined to compromise. The American Medical Association sensed which way the wind was blowing and backed away from their opposition to the mandatory provision of medical benefits by employers.

As expected, Congress in 1975 was a more liberal body than it had been before. Seventy-five new Democrats were elected to the House, many of them liberal and committed to the Griffiths-Corman plan. Under other circumstances this should have made passage of a strong national health insurance bill possible. But budgetary and economic developments led Ford to abandon his earlier support for national health insurance. In early 1975 Ford announced a moratorium on new spending proposals. Secretary Weinberger did promise that the administration would resubmit a health insurance proposal in 1976, by which time the administration expected that the economy would have improved.

Given the difficulties of 1974, with Nixon's extended political crisis and the arrival of Gerald Ford as the new president, it may have been impossible under the best of circumstances to adopt a dramatic new health initiative that year. But the efforts of Democratic constituencies to avoid a compromise certainly made a difficult task far harder. By 1975 Senator Kennedy may have realized that the middle of the road was a dangerous place, for he abandoned the compromise proposal he sponsored with Mills in 1974 and was back on board with Griffiths and Corman.

National health insurance was not adopted in 1974 or 1975, but

Democrats probably looked hopefully to the election of a Democratic president in 1976 under whose leadership a comprehensive health care bill could be adopted. What they could not understand was that 1976 marked the closing of a window of opportunity. As David Mayhew argues, an activist public mood that had begun around 1960 was ending, and was replaced by a new conservative mood that did not favor the enactment of big new social schemes.[56] The failure of much of Jimmy Carter's agenda despite huge Democratic majorities in Congress stands as testimony to the changed political atmosphere.

Kennedy, Carter, and National Health Insurance

In the Carter administration, there once again arose an opportunity to pass health care legislation. As before, the president's proposals fell short of what policy activists sought. Also as before, an unwillingness to accept a compromise doomed legislation that, while imperfect, was better than nothing.

We normally expect that having a president and a Congress of the same party will tend to reduce interbranch conflict, but that is not necessarily the case, as a 1978 dispute between President Carter and Senator Edward Kennedy over health care confirmed. Harmony is to be expected if there is substantial unity of interest between the president and members of his party in Congress. Often that is the case, because Democratic members generally want a Democratic president to be popular and successful, if only because they fear backlash against an unpopular president in midterm elections. Members of the president's party will not agree with him on everything, but they are not normally motivated to harm the president. Those who disagree with the president's legislative program doubtlessly will voice their views. And if the president is terribly unpopular, they will naturally distance themselves. But even when members of the president's party want to maintain some distance, it does not help them to hurt the president. Generally speaking, if the president does well and is popular, other members of his party do well. American parties are famously loose in their organization, but Democrats nonetheless see some common destiny that binds them together, however loosely.

Whether it controls Congress or not, the opposition party has an incentive to harm the president and defeat his legislative program. (There are also some countervailing incentives to compromise to pass legislation of mutual benefit.) The opposition is commonly presented with opportunities to harm the president and ruin his reputation, and thereby help itself in the next election. Thus in April 1993, Senate Republicans filibustered President Clinton's economic stimulus package and denounced it for wastefulness, not because it was such a major issue for them, but because it seemed to be good politics to interfere with the president's program.[57]

When members of Congress from the president's party are trying to steal the party's presidential nomination from the incumbent, their incentives are essentially identical to those of the opposition party: whatever hurts the president helps them. This accounts for the competition on health care that occurred between Carter and Kennedy. Kennedy sought to retain his position as the leader on health care, and to do this he deliberately avoided an agreement with Carter.

Because he was running for the 1980 Democratic presidential nomination (even though his candidacy was not yet announced), Kennedy behaved toward Carter precisely as if Carter were a Republican, an enemy whose success could only hurt Kennedy. Kennedy picked fights, misrepresented administration policies, magnified differences, and presented competing legislation as he courted the liberal wing of the Democratic party. The goal was to damage Carter's presidency and win the nomination for himself.

Carter had endorsed national health insurance as a candidate, but later backed away as inflation rose and budget deficits proved intractable.[58] Instead of a comprehensive plan, Carter offered piecemeal reform, which gave Kennedy a chance to take the liberal high ground and discredit Carter among important constituencies, especially organized labor. Kennedy insisted that the president endorse his comprehensive proposal, which would cost perhaps $100 billion, and which was totally contrary to Carter's plans to balance the budget and fight inflation. By endorsing a proposal that Carter could not accept, Kennedy showed how he and the president differed on an issue of great concern to Democratic activists. According to Jody Powell,

> this placed us in an awkward position. If we tried to cuddle up to Kennedy on issues such as national health insurance, we would increase our vulnerability from the center and right, thus lending credence to Kennedy's "political weakness" argument. If we stuck to our guns, he would continue to accuse us of insensitivity to the poor, exacerbate our difficulties with Democratic interest groups, and claim that in the end these problems had forced him into the race.[59]

Carter's Department of Health, Education, and Welfare, under the secretaryship of Joseph Califano, drew up an administration health plan and a list of principles. Carter favored moving slowly toward national health insurance, not only because of budgetary concerns but also because he considered it unlikely that a comprehensive plan could be enacted at that time. In a White House meeting that amounted to a showdown between Kennedy and Carter, the president explained his preference for submitting several bills rather than a single bill. Kennedy insisted that only a single bill would suffice.[60]

Califano reports that an hour after the meeting Kennedy called him, saying he was besieged by members of the press who wanted to know the outcome of the meeting. Kennedy wanted to have a press conference. Califano asked him to delay for one day until the administration could finalize its own plans and have a press conference to announce its health care reform principles. Kennedy refused to wait: "There's just too much furor over this," he told Califano.[61] That afternoon Kennedy held his press conference. Surrounded by leaders of major labor unions and senior citizen groups, he denounced Carter for a "failure of leadership" on the issue. He described a "fundamental difference" between his position and Carter's, and announced that he would introduce his own legislation, based on a single bill rather than several, that would move more quickly and unhesitatingly toward national health insurance.[62] In a speech to the AMA he said: "The President and his economic advisors, and the Secretary of HEW want to launch a ship of national health insurance with a hole beneath the waterline. . . . Now that we have parted ways with the administration, our coalition will develop its own proposals."[63]

Kennedy's behavior appears to have been deliberately calculated to provoke a break with the administration, which he then did everything in his power to publicize. Kennedy's behavior appears to have been designed to transfer the support of organized labor and other constituencies interested in national health insurance from Carter to himself. It is unlikely that his goal was actually to pass a bill, since he had been unable for ten years running to get a bill of this kind out of his Senate committee. Moreover, Al Ullman, chairman of the House Ways and Means Committee, and Russell Long, chairman of the Senate Finance Committee, were both opposed to a comprehensive bill.[64]

To counter the threat from Kennedy, Carter might have endorsed a comprehensive proposal. Powell reports that among Kennedy staff members, "the greatest fear was that we would capitulate, adopt all his proposals, and then stand back while they died aborning in Congress."[65] This did not happen, and could not happen, because Carter's number one priority in 1977 and 1978 was his war against inflation, a goal that could not be reconciled with support for a new and expensive health initiative.

No bill passed, but the dispute increased press perceptions that

Carter was incompetent in his dealings with Congress, and certainly helped advance Kennedy's presidential efforts. A little more than a year later he announced he would challenge Carter for the Democratic nomination, a challenge that might well have been successful had the Iran hostage crisis not boosted Carter's sagging popularity. Kennedy's strategy of avoiding an agreement with Carter over health care was good politics, though it did help to prevent the enactment of Carter's more modest health care bill.[66]

Opportunities to pass health care legislation presented themselves repeatedly over the past decades, as a disadvantaged party sought to gain ground on its opponent. The efforts of the advantaged party have nearly as often kept legislation from passing.

Social Security under Nixon

When two or more groups battle for advantage with an important constituency, a bidding war can result. The politics of Social Security benefit increases in the first term of the Nixon presidency, especially the increase passed in 1972, provides a prototype of the bidding-up phenomenon. In an effort to secure the loyalty and votes of the elderly, presidential candidates in the Democratic party and President Richard Nixon managed to escalate Social Security benefit increases, producing a 23 percent increase in the real value of benefits over the period 1969 to 1972. Democrats sought to capitalize on their advantage in Social Security, but President Nixon, who was nothing if not politically shrewd, was unwilling to be outdone. He proposed increases, Congress regularly passed larger ones than recommended, but Nixon signed anything Congress sent him. Martha Derthick describes the relationship between President Nixon and the Democratic Congress: "Party rivalry in a divided government was one cause of this extraordinary escalation. The Republican administration consistently proposed benefit increases in proportion to increases in the cost of living, and the Democratic Congress consistently outbid it, raising the Republican offer in 1969 from 10 to 15 percent, in 1971 from 6 to 10 percent, and in 1972 from 5 to 20 percent."[67] Robert J. Myers also sees the cause of the large run-up in benefits in divided government:

> Why then has all this expansion occurred, especially when an Administration was in office that has professed to be conservative or moderate in social and economic philosophy? One reason has been the unfortunate situation of the Executive Branch being controlled by one political party and the Legislative Branch being controlled by the other one. This has produced an unhealthy political competition, with each party trying to outbid the other.[68]

Eliot Richardson, Nixon's secretary of HEW, also saw an inevitable bidding war between branches of the government over Social Security: "I think it is a commonplace that the interaction of the executive and the legislative branches of government often produces a desirable resultant of the competing forces. It is obvious further, I think, that a Republican President could expect in many situations like this to be outbid no matter what he might propose, and, of course, this has happened again and again."[69]

Raising Social Security benefits was a standard and honored practice in American politics for much of the postwar period. As inflation eroded the value of benefits, it gave politicians an excuse to pass a bill to restore the lost value, which they did with great regularity. Although the ostensible logic was to prevent the erosion of Social Security benefits, the logic of election year politics often, even usually, led to the enactment of a bill that actually raised benefits in real terms so that benefits would keep up with increases in wages.

Wilbur Mills, Democrat of Arkansas and chairman of the House Ways and Means Committee, occupies a prominent place in any story of Social Security policy making. In 1969 the Nixon administration requested a 7 percent cost-of-living increase; this was opposed by Mills, who preferred to act on Social Security in 1970 when the Ways and Means calendar would be less crowded. Nixon sought an increase in 1969, which was not an election year, in hopes that Congress would not have to deal with Social Security in 1970 when election pressures would tend to push the increase up. Nixon also sought the adoption of an automatic inflation adjustment as a means of preventing biennial extravaganzas. When fifty-three members of the House cosponsored legislation calling for a 15 percent increase, Mills prudently decided not to wait until 1970 and managed to work Social Security into the busy Ways and Means schedule before the end of the year. Ways and Means unanimously supported a 15 percent increase in benefits. Recognizing that his 7 percent proposal was a loser, Nixon offered 10 percent as a compromise. But Congress attached the Social Security legislation to a veto-proof tax bill, which ensured its passage.

In 1970 the Nixon administration again sought to obtain the enactment of an automatic cost-of-living allowance (COLA) in order to prevent the kind of increase that had occurred just the year before. It recommended a benefit increase of 5 percent and the enactment of an automatic COLA that would be triggered when the CPI rose 3 percent. Mills opposed the COLA provisions, but the House voted for them on the floor. The House bill thus very closely resembled the administration's request. The Senate bill called for a 10 percent increase, and before the two chambers could resolve their differences, the Congress ended.

In 1971 work on Social Security continued apace. The Nixon administration renewed its campaign for an automatic COLA, recommending both it and a 6 percent benefit increase. Compensating for its dereliction in not passing a bill in 1970, Congress got to work quickly and passed a bill providing a 10 percent increase in benefits and attached it to a veto-proof debt ceiling bill. It was signed by the president on March 16. In April, Mills relented on the COLA issue. The Ways and Means Committee included another 5 percent increase in benefits with this legislation. But it did not pass because the Senate failed to act.

As the 1972 session opened, the House bill with its 5 percent increase and COLA provisions was still pending. But Wilbur Mills shocked the Washington political community by calling in February for a 20 percent increase in benefits, although inflation had risen by only 7 percent since the previous bill. This action by Mills, who had previously served as a conservative influence in Social Security politics, deserves some explanation. Several different influences were no doubt at work, but two of them will receive special attention here: the switch from the level earnings assumption to dynamic earnings, and the emergence of Wilbur Mills's presidential aspirations.

For purposes of calculating the "actuarial soundness" of the Social Security system, various assumptions must be made regarding such matters as the life expectancy of recipients and the total value of future income subject to Social Security taxes. The former assumption is crucial in determining the likely cost of the program in the future, and the latter in ascertaining the funds available to meet Social Security liabilities. The object, of course, is to provide a balance in the program whereby long-term costs match long-term revenues. For many years the Social Security Admistration (SSA) had employed what was termed the level earnings assumption. That is, in calculating the soundness of the system, it was assumed that the payroll subject to Social Security taxes would not grow. This was an assumption of profound political ramifications, for if one instead assumed that earnings would grow at an annual rate of 3 percent, then revenues would grow substantially in the future. And if next year's revenue is higher than this year's, it means that any surpluses accumulated in the trust fund could be distributed to recipients in the form of higher benefits.

Use of the level earnings assumption tended to increase real benefits in the long run, for it implied that increases in real wage levels justified equivalent increases in benefits. When wages rose (always unexpectedly, given the level earnings assumption), the SSA would "discover" a surplus in the Social Security system, which justified a benefit increase.[70]

The shift to indexation of benefits through a COLA required abandoning the level earnings assumption in favor of dynamic earnings. If Social Security benefits were to be tied to prices, it then had to be assumed that wages (and Social Security receipts) would at least keep pace with inflation. Robert J. Myers, the chief SSA actuary, was opposed to any such alteration in the earnings assumption, particularly because he believed that reliance on a dynamic earnings assumption would produce "actuarial gains" that would be used to fund liberalizations of benefits. This approach he found risky and imprudent, largely because the size of any actuarial gain was extremely sensitive to assumptions of future earnings growth.[71] He also warned of the "hidden hazard" of declining birth rates.[72] Had Myers remained in his position as chief actuary it would have been difficult to adopt the dynamic earnings approach, but he left the government in 1970.

This somewhat tedious discussion of assumptions is necessary to understand some of what was to follow. Use of dynamic earnings had been advocated for a number of years by outside critics and was finally adopted, not for the reasons suggested by economists, but because it was consistent with an automatic COLA. Within the Nixon administration, a possibly unforeseen side effect of dynamic earnings was to produce a large one-time actuarial surplus that could be used to increase benefits. This created a good deal of uncertainty among entrepreneurial politicians. In taking advantage of this new surplus created by a bookkeeping change, how much of an increase should they propose? And how much of an increase would their rivals propose?

The second important factor in explaining Mills's suddenly incautious behavior was his urge to be president. Although extremely powerful by virtue of his great influence within the Ways and Means

Committee, Mills was nonetheless relatively unknown to the larger public. He must have seen that being in the vanguard of those calling for higher Social Security benefits could earn him at least some of the visibility and support he needed to make a run for national office. The dynamic earnings assumption would hurt Democrats in the long run (assuming they maintained control of Congress) for it would deprive them of their traditional excuse to boost benefits. But the one-time surplus generated from the transition could redound very much to Mills's benefit.

Hence, Mills increased his proposed boost in Social Security benefits from 5 to 20 percent. Why did he propose such a large increase over the president's proposal of a 5 percent increase? Although only Mills knows his true motivations, it seems likely that a desire to upstage the president and to avoid losing the Social Security issue to members of his own party contributed to his action. According to Derthick, "as a legislative leader, [Mills] was adroit at anticipating political pressure. Perhaps in 1972 he anticipated a bold initiative by the politician in the White House, who, he may well have supposed, would be irresistibly tempted by an actuarial windfall in social security in a year when his own office was at stake."[73] Moreover, he had politicians in his own party to worry about as well. George McGovern and Frank Church, both also contenders for the Democratic nomination, suggested a 20 percent increase even before Mills did. Hubert Humphrey proposed 25 percent. To recommend less than 20 percent would have sacrificed leadership on the issue.

For such forthright liberals as McGovern and Church to urge a 20 percent increase was not at all out of character, but it was for Mills. He had a well-deserved reputation as a careful and deliberate man, not given to excess. He was, moreover, both attached to the level earnings assumption and fully aware of its significance.[74] So it is perplexing that Mills would so gladly embrace the dynamic earnings assumption and the benefit increases it permitted without careful study and without hearings. Mills the presidential candidate was a fundamentally different political creature than Mills the inside operator. As a presidential candidate he had to take actions that would appeal to large constituencies; that need drove him to champion policies he would previously have rejected, or at least adopted only after long and careful study.

Nixon did not like the size of the increase, primarily because he was in the midst of a major battle against spending (soon he would begin his series of impoundments), and seriously considered vetoing the bill. Advisers within the White House, sensitive to the importance of the elderly vote, pressured Nixon to sign the bill despite his misgivings.[75] Once having decided to accept the Democratic bidding up of Social Security benefits, the administration did its best to get as much credit as possible for the increase. Since 1954 Social Security checks including new benefit increases have carried a notice informing the recipient that "Congress has passed and the President has signed" a bill responsible for the windfall.[76] According to Robert Ball, then SSA commissioner, the Nixon administration sought to violate previous custom and give Congress no credit. By threatening to resign, Ball got the administration to use the standard language.[77]

Disadvantaged parties and politicians pursue agreements that will minimize differences, and advantaged parties avoid them. And so in some cases legislation fails that might otherwise pass. Or in other cases the bargaining causes legislation that probably should not be passed to win with overwhelming support from all sides. The bargaining follows a logic that makes sense given the political stakes of the bargainers, but which is otherwise perverse.

3   The Strategy of Encroachment

The only way to get
some pie is a slice at a time.
—*Carl Elliott, Sr.*

This chapter explores a situation similar to strategic pursuit and avoidance, but with an important difference. It covers instances where no zone of potential agreement exists, but where the disadvantaged party is interested in providing the appearance that the two sides are closer together than they really are. In cases of strategic encroachment, the opponents of a legislative proposal recognize that it has great public appeal and do not want to be seen as foot draggers or naysayers, but at the same time, they would rather avoid having any bill pass. To escape blame for killing a popular program or idea, members of the disadvantaged party forward proposals that position them relatively close to the advantaged party, but at the same time take steps to ensure that their proposals do not become law. The overriding goal is to minimize the opponents' political advantages in an issue area by blurring the distinctiveness of respective positions.

The best way of obscuring distinctions between parties is by passing a bill, but this option is sometimes unavailable, as when the disadvantaged party is deeply split, or when important constituents would rebel at the passage of legislation. As chapter 2 explains, persuading politicians to act strategically can be a problem, for many of them may refuse to believe that a problem exists. Encroachment is a defensive strategy for the disadvantaged party that requires less action and less internal agreement, for it does not require the party to unify behind a proposal and pass it.

Encroachment can work to draw off support from the leading alternative, leaving none with a majority. This strategy can succeed because there is typically a range of opinion within the supporting coalition. Some will think the leading proposal is too limited, while others consider it about right. Still others, however, will be willing to vote for the bill even though they do not like it, because they recognize that many voters are interested in seeing something done. Such representatives may have serious objections to the legislation but, lacking confidence that they can explain these objections to their voters, they are inclined to vote for the bill, considering that the course of least resistance.

To keep fence-sitters from voting for a bill, the disadvantaged party must provide them with something else they can vote for. In a 1959 cabinet discussion of aid to education, Nixon argued that the Republican party could not flatly oppose school construction because, he said, "Nothing hits people more directly than their kids in school," and "we cannot win on this issue by saying 'there is no need' or that 'the need will soon be met.'"[1] Nixon argued that it was important for the administration to take a positive position on the issue even though the majority of the Republican congressional leadership, and most of the rest of the members, would be opposed. "You will find," he said, "that the people who are 'for' are the ones from the closest districts. These are the ones for whom this is a problem. . . . If we do not put up a program, we must give these fellows a position they can take without going along on the $5 billion level the opposition is putting up." HEW Secretary Arthur Flemming added: "That is why we need a positive program. I do not like to see these men left out in the cold without such a position."[2] Having a program may prevent Republicans in close districts from supporting the Democratic bill. Meanwhile, the hard-core conservatives who favor

doing nothing vote against everything, and do so proudly. If successful, this strategy produces a three-way split in the vote among liberals, conservatives, and moderates, with none getting a majority.
Equally important, it obscures the position of many opponents and
permits them to claim some credit in the policy area.

In 1994, putting forward a specious alternative helped Democrats
kill a popular constitutional amendment to require a balanced federal
budget. Some Democrats who opposed the constitutional amendment nonetheless faced great pressure to vote for it, if only because
a nay vote could readily be interpreted by electoral opponents as support for budget deficits. In both the House and Senate, opponents
of the balanced budget amendment crafted a weaker alternative they
did not want to see enacted, solely to siphon off support from the
more stringent balanced budget proposal. In the Senate, the stringent amendment was four votes short of passing; seven Democrats
voted for the weaker alternative and against the serious proposal. In
the House, the amendment was twelve votes short of passing; sixty-
four Democrats voted for the alternative but against the stronger
amendment proposal.[3]

Family leave legislation was a potent issue in 1991 and 1992, for
it was an issue that allowed Democrats to take a pro-family position
and put Republicans on the defensive. The Democratic bill required
businesses to allow employees to take twelve weeks of unpaid leave
to care for a new baby or a sick relative—a position most voters
supported, but which Republicans were largely unable to support
since it violated their free market principles. Republicans offered a
substitute amendment that was widely seen as "an effort to give
members of Congress something 'pro-family' to vote for."[4] Supporters of the original bill called the substitute a "Trojan horse." The
substitute did not draw off enough votes to defeat the bill, but it
kept enough votes in the "no" column to sustain President Bush's
veto.

This tactic can be very important under divided party government. A Republican president can normally check Democratic enthusiasm by means of the veto, but an important job for the president's party in Congress is to spare the president that unpleasant and politically costly necessity. They can do this by working to keep any bill from passing. As legislation to provide federal aid to education was working its way through Congress in 1960, a very high priority in the White House was to prevent the enactment of a bill the president would be forced to veto.[5] An administration plan existed for the purpose of drawing off moderate support, which it did. No bill passed due to the unwillingness of various factions to compromise. One problem in this strategy is that while the president wants Republicans in Congress to kill the bill, those very Republicans may want to be able to vote for the liberal bill and then count on the president to kill it with a veto. If there is very great pressure on members of Congress to vote for the leading alternative, the president may not be able to persuade his party in Congress to take the heat. But the advantage of killing the bill in Congress by dividing support is that no one needs to be the villain.

Killing all legislation by offering an alternative proposal depends on the actions and preferences of the moderates in both parties. For this strategy to work, there must be a group of moderate swing representatives who want to vote for some form of legislation but are reluctant to support legislation offered by liberal Democrats. Let us assume that the liberals in the Democratic party favor vigorous legislation and oppose a compromise measure. The moderates in the Democratic party want to pass a bill but are somewhat hesitant to support the liberal Democrats' bill, believing that less is needed. Moderates in the Republican party are likewise reluctant to support the Democratic bill because, while they support doing something, they do not want to do much. The Republican conservatives favor doing nothing at all. A Republican president under these conditions faces a dilemma. If he tries to help moderates in his party by passing a moderate bill, he may split the party. But if the president opposes all legislation, moderate legislators, especially those in marginal districts, may bolt and support the liberal bill as a way of showing their districts that they are on the right side of the issue. Such support from moderate representatives might actually provide the margin of victory for the liberal bill, helping it get out of Congress and to the president's desk, where he must either sign a distasteful bill or veto it, accepting the attendant political costs.

In another scenario, the Democrats are generally in favor of doing something, but too divided among themselves to pass a bill. The Republicans issue a proposal, not to subvert the Democrats, but to ensure that they do not appear totally negative. In this stage of "policy germination" there are typically a large number of proposals floating around, competing for support, without any emerging as a leader. But if the Democrats are the only ones floating proposals, the public may associate only Democrats with the goal and give them credit in the issue. In such cases the president may unveil a proposal, not with any expectation that it will become law, but to give Republicans in Congress a standard around which to rally, a bill for them to point to in their campaigns should they find it convenient. Issuing a proposal immunizes a president somewhat against charges that he is doing nothing about said problem, and allows him to shift the blame to Congress, which the president can point out is doing nothing. Whenever the issue comes up the president can point to his program and blame Congress for not acting on it. In the 1992 presidential campaign health care loomed large as an issue, even though neither party had nearly the unity necessary to pass any significant legislation. President Bush faced no danger of having to veto a popular bill, but he still issued his own health care proposal (which no one expected to pass), primarily because it was bad to be without a plan. Members of Congress could not so easily blame inaction on a lack of leadership from the White House, even though the president did virtually nothing to support his own proposal.

In both of these cases, whether the Republicans adopt a position or issue a proposal, the purpose is not to pass a bill but to keep the Democrats from getting exclusive credit for promoting a popular issue. The president announces his plan, which is endorsed by as many Republicans as think it will benefit them. Others can criticize the president or say nothing.

The advantaged party has defenses against these efforts to obscure differences. In some cases of strategic encroachment, many members of the disadvantaged party may be solidly opposed to legislation in the policy area in question; but they support their party position to keep from seeming too negative, and because they are confident that no legislation will pass. In such cases, an excellent defense is for the advantaged party to embrace the opposition proposal. This can cause total panic in the ranks of the disadvantaged party. Legislators who supported their party position in the expectation that it would lose must then scramble to keep the bill from passing and to avoid the appearance that they are fighting their own bill. Such accommodation by the Democrats has its risks as well. If it turns out that sufficient numbers of Republicans do support their proposal, the addition of Democratic votes might help it pass. If so, the Democrats are big losers, for the distinction between the two parties is wiped out and the adoption of reformist legislation can prevent adoption of stronger legislation in the future. Of course, it may genuinely be the case that the Democrats have concluded that a bill is better than an issue (sometimes otherwise quixotic liberals do reach this conclusion), and that if the Republican bill is the only one that will pass, they will support it. Before lending their support to a bill they do not want to pass, the disadvantaged party should be sure that their opponent is in no mood to compromise.

One's expectations about the other side's intentions determines choice of tactics. If Republicans are sure that Democrats will accept no compromise, they are free to snuggle up very close to the Democratic position without worrying that a bill they oppose will inadvertently become law. If Democrats think Republicans are bluffing, they can propose compromises they do not want to see implemented. A high degree of uncertainty about the other party's intentions is likely to discourage risky tactical maneuvering.

If it appears that the Republicans are united behind the idea of passing a halfway measure in order to diminish the difference between the parties, the Democrats cannot call the bluff, since there is no bluff. If they are interested in enacting a bill, even if imperfect, this provides an excellent opportunity. But if they prefer the issue to the bill, a better approach here is to call attention to the miserable inadequacy of the Republican measure and encourage interest group leaders to ridicule it. The constant goal of the Democrats in this position must be to prevent their more conservative colleagues from becoming unduly pragmatic and accepting the Republican position on the grounds that "it's the best we can get," for such thinking dooms Democratic strategy.

Aid to Education Politics in 1956 and 1957

The legislative battle over federal aid to education in 1957 presents the classic instance of strategic encroachment, with the Republicans trying to steal some thunder by offering a proposal that was quite close to the Democratic position. We know it was a fake offer because, when the Democrats unexpectedly agreed to the Republican plan and it threatened to pass, the Republicans disowned it—and in doing so revealed their strategy.[6]

The issue of federal aid to education, seemingly innocuous today, was contentious from the early 1950s through 1965. At issue was whether the federal government should help states and localities build elementary and secondary schools to accommodate the rapidly growing school age population. These proposals aroused intense feelings among liberals and conservatives alike—the conservatives fearing that federal involvement with local schools would eventually mean federal control, and the liberals believing that federal assistance was crucial to solving an education crisis. The issue arose repeatedly, and Congress sought to pass legislation nearly every year from 1954 onward, not succeeding until 1965.[7]

The standard interpretation among both scholars and participants, propagated especially by William Riker, holds that the Powell amendment killed school construction by alienating vital Southern Democratic votes.[8] Powell or a helpful Republican offered amendments barring aid to segregated schools in 1956 and 1957, and in both years they passed with the support of Republicans and northern Democrats. In 1956 the bill was voted down for final passage, and in 1957 it was killed by a procedural vote.[9] In this story it is assumed that there was a majority to pass a bill uncorrupted by the Powell amendment, composed of Democrats and liberal Republicans. When the Powell amendment passed, Southern Democrats who would otherwise have supported the bill voted against it, since their states could get no money from it.

The Republicans learned from the aid for education fight in 1956 to expect intransigence from the Democrats, and this emboldened them to encroach strategically upon the Democratic position in 1957. In 1956 the Democrats prepared school legislation and brought it to the floor. It being an election year, the Republicans were eager to avoid political damage on the subject and may actually have been interested in passing a bill, albeit one more modest than the Democratic proposal. On the floor they offered two amendments to scale back the Democratic bill, but both of these were defeated. The House then went on to adopt Powell's antisegregation amendment and reported the bill to the House proper, where Republicans and Southern Democrats joined forces to vote it down.

Judging from comments in a legislative strategy session, it appears that in 1956 Republicans were interested in passing a bill but thought—correctly, it seems—that Democrats would be unwilling to compromise. Responding to a question from Eisenhower, Joe Martin said he would try to restart the administration's bill but doubted it could be passed because, he said, "the Democrats were not going to do anything in this election year that would put the Republicans in a good light."[10]

The Republicans assumed that Democrats would not compromise in order to pass a bill because 1956 was a presidential election year, and they were not about to give up a good issue the summer before an election. But they were mistaken in expecting similar inflexibility in 1957, when the Democrats had been soundly defeated and the next election was four years away.

One may reasonably wonder why the Republicans showed so much interest in a legislative proposal that was so antithetical to their ideology at the time. Even Eisenhower, who appears to have been one of the stronger supporters among Republicans, was very uneasy about the idea. But two motivations appear to explain Republican activities. First, there was a conviction among some that the classroom shortage was real and that local school districts would not be able to build enough without some outside help; second, there was a concern that Republican candidates would be harmed if their party appeared to be against the increasingly popular idea of federal aid to education. "The people see a crisis," Nixon explained in a strategy meeting. "It will be very bad for our candidates in close districts if they oppose any action."[11]

No legislation passed in 1956 but Eisenhower endorsed aid to education again in 1957. To help the legislation, Eisenhower gave at least three major speeches supporting it. After some delay, Representative Graham Barden, Democrat of North Carolina and chairman of the House Education and Labor Committee, held hearings and a markup. In committee, an antisegregation amendment was offered but defeated.

The committee began its work with a substantially more far-reaching bill than the administration wanted, but a compromise left only two significant differences: the administration wanted $200 million less in spending and a distribution formula that would target aid to states with the greatest need. Nonetheless, Eisenhower endorsed the committee bill, telling a Republican supporter of the bill that "you will have my full support. Something must be done."[12]

Despite the endorsement, the White House waffled endlessly, sending a series of confusing messages that puzzled supporters and encouraged opponents. On June 12 he invited forty Republicans to the White House for breakfast, ostensibly to lobby them on school aid and other bills before Congress. It was an odd sort of lobbying, however, for when an Ohio Republican said he would be hung in his district if he voted for the school bill, the president expressed his own ambivalence about the legislation, and said he hoped the program, if enacted, would expire before he left office.[13] Since the committee bill authorized the program for five years, it would clearly last beyond the end of Eisenhower's second term. Even Eisenhower's bill would continue into the next administration, so his comment set off rumors that he wanted the bill cut down to three years' duration. These reports were denied by the White House, but they left a distinct impression of soft support from the president.[14] Representative Peter Freylinghuysen, Republican of New York, wrote to Eisenhower asking his position on the bill. Eisenhower responded: "I earnestly hope . . . that legislation will be enacted at this session to provide Federal help in this emergency."[15] This is hardly the language a president keen on seeing a bill enacted would use. He noted that the Republican platform had pledged the party to school construction legislation and that there was a need for more classrooms, but he did not urge Republicans to vote for the bill. In early July Vice President Nixon delivered a message from the president to the national convention of the NEA. "Nothing is more important to the future of this nation," he said, "than the proper education of our children." He then went on to deplore the inadequacy of school facilities and the failure of Congress to authorize assistance for school construction in the past, which, he noted, he had "repeatedly urged" them to do.[16] On the other hand, Republican leaders reported that the president was "not entirely satisfied" with the bill reported from committee but was willing to accept it "as a start." Joe Martin said that the bill's chances were not bright but said the president did want a bill.[17] Shortly before the bill went to the House floor, Secretary of HEW Marion Folsom went to see the president, apparently hoping to get a presidential commitment to actively support the bill by making telephone calls on its behalf. He was disappointed.[18]

In floor debate, Powell himself did not offer an antisegregation amendment, since he was on the French Riviera at the time, but a New York Republican, Stuyvesant Wainwright, offered it in his absence. It passed again, no doubt supported by the same coalition of Republicans and northern Democrats that had passed it the previous year. This action would almost certainly have doomed any possibility of enacting school construction assistance in 1957. At this point Republicans interested only in defeating the bill could have rested assured that on the vote for final passage they would have the help of Southern Democrats in voting it down. That, however, would have left the Republicans looking entirely negative on the question of school construction. Their desire to seem constructive, combined with an unwillingness to go along with wild Democratic schemes, led them to offer and initially support an amendment that placed them quite close to the Democratic position.

Representative William Ayres, Republican of Ohio, offered a substitute amendment that would replace the entire committee bill with legislation the administration had proposed and supported in 1956, and continued to support in 1957. This amendment would implement the distribution ratio and the four-year duration favored by the administration. In fact, it would give the administration exactly what it had asked for. Republican leaders took the floor to praise the Ayres amendment. Charles Halleck warmly endorsed the Ayres amendment: "I commend the gentleman from Ohio for offering this substitute. It is President Eisenhower's program. I voted for it last year and I shall support the substitute this year."[19] It was also essentially the same amendment that McConnell had offered in 1956 without attracting Democratic support.

But in 1957 the situation was quite different, for the next presidential election was not until 1960, and the benefits to Democrats in avoiding an agreement were small. The preelection intransigence of the Democrats was replaced by a postelection desire to see a bill enacted. The Republican amendment was a substitute, a proposal to eliminate the entire Democratic bill, including the Wainwright-Powell amendment. Understanding that the committee bill, burdened by the desegregation amendment, had no chance, liberal Democrats capitulated and announced their support for the Ayres amendment. Representative Lee Metcalf, Democrat of Montana, expressed the new Democratic position well: "I feel we need to get a school bill. I have compromised as much as 75 percent of the way, and I see no reason why I should not compromise 100 percent of the way. I accept the Eisenhower bill in its entirety."[20] This was the only route to an education bill in 1957 and the liberals decided to take it. With conservatives like Halleck and the liberal wing of the Democratic party supporting the same amendment, its passage seemed inevitable. Asked if a Powell-type amendment would be offered to his substitute, Ayres said he understood that the amendment would not be offered again.[21] This was truly a great opportunity for passing the bill!

Republican leaders were chagrined at this turn of events, and were "nearly caught flat-footed by the switch in Democratic strategy," for they did not really want their own amendment to pass.[22] In endorsing the Ayres amendment Republicans were apparently confident that the Democrats would refuse to give their ground and that the amendment would fail, after which the entire bill could be voted down. To rescue the situation, and to keep the amendment from passing, Halleck went into conference with "Judge" Howard Smith, a conservative Southern Democrat who was also chair of the Rules Committee. Meanwhile, Democratic supporters of the bill stalled for time, trying to enlist the support of the president. Smith moved to strike the enacting clause.[23] This tactic was chosen because the motion to strike the enacting clause takes precedence over a pending amendment, and if it passed would save Republicans who wanted to kill the bill from having to vote directly against the substitute. The motion passed in the Committee of the Whole.

Following this vote the House itself had to vote on the motion to strike, giving supporters of the bill time to rally the president to the cause. They tried to contact Eisenhower to enlist his support, but he was unavailable. No comments or encouragement came from the White House. The unavailability of Eisenhower at that crucial moment must mean that he did not want to be reached. An examination of his schedule shows that for all of July 25 he was either in his office or hitting golf balls on the White House grounds; he had no meetings with heads of state or other events so important that they could not be interrupted.[24] With no words of support forthcoming from the White House, the House of Representatives went on to vote to strike the enacting clause, 208–203.

After the bill's demise, Democrats grumbled about Eisenhower's absence from the fight, asserting that his voice would have made the difference. Republican leaders in the House also agreed that more forceful involvement by the president would have swung the vote.[25] In a presidential press conference, Edward Folliard of the *Washington Post* asked about the events. Democrats "were willing to go along with your bill," he said, "and their complaint is that you failed to go to bat for the legislation. . . . They said had you spoken up the legislation would have passed." Eisenhower's reply is bewildering, for he essentially denied the events of the week before. "I never heard that, Mr. Folliard," he said. "If that is true, why are you telling me something I never heard?" Eisenhower went on to say that he had spoken up for the bill many times and even given speeches on its behalf. But he believed that "you don't influence Congress, in my opinion, by threats. . . . I try to win their votes over, but I don't get up and make statements every twenty minutes."[26] Then he promised to send another education bill to Congress the next year.

The fight over school aid in 1957 is a fascinating and puzzling episode. Was the Republican offer of its education plan, very similar to the Democratic plan, nothing but a political ploy? Did they have no intention of its passing? Or did Eisenhower seek the bill's passage only to be frustrated by the connivance of conservatives in Congress? It is very much an open question what Eisenhower thought of the 1957 school construction bill and whether he wanted it to pass. His behavior and statements on the issue are so full of contradictions that one can find evidence both of his firm support for the bill and of his uncertainty about the wisdom of the bill.

Evidence of his support is plentiful. He gave speeches on the subject. He said publicly that he would sign the House bill if it reached his desk, even though he preferred his own bill. The day after the education bill failed, Ann Whitman wrote in her diary: "The president distressed at the Republican members of Congress who vote against him; asked me to be sure that any one that asks for a favor for a constituent or himself—that his voting record is attached to the request as it comes to him for decision."[27] Evidence of ambivalence about the bill is equally abundant. On the very day he was so angered by his party's disloyalty, he himself had done nothing to help the education bill. Days before he refused the request of Marion Folsom to make phone calls on behalf of the bill. It is one thing for a president to say he supports a bill and another to try to sway votes. In the breakfast meeting he said he wanted the program to expire before he left office, yet none of the pending proposals would have expired before the end of his term. By expressing contradictory views on the bill, and by doing nothing to secure its passage, Eisenhower communicated to Republicans, inadvertently or not, that they should vote however they pleased. Furthermore, in discussing the 1958 Defense Education Act, Eisenhower said he had been forced to support the 1957 bill against his will, and that the only school construction bill he truly liked was a minimal approach advocated by his first HEW secretary, Oveta Culp Hobby.

But whatever one believes Eisenhower actually wanted, the sum consequence of his behavior was highly strategic. The public position of the administration was clear, as both the president and vice president had uttered liberal sentiments on the subject. The Republican platform had called for school aid and the president had acted on the platform. The actions of Eisenhower protected the Republican party from charges that it ignored the young of America; at the same time he avoided a battle with the right wing of the Republican party by not insisting that anyone follow the official administration line. Its equivocation allowed the administration to be all things to all people—liberal to those who wanted it to be liberal and conservative to those who wanted it to be conservative. This was an excellent strategy and it failed only because the Democrats proved unexpectedly willing to compromise.

Hubert Humphrey Tries to Ban the Communist Party

Senator Hubert Humphrey, Democrat of Minnesota, was responsible for an audacious and awe-inspiring encroachment on the Republican stronghold of anticommunism. Concerned that the public considered the Democratic party "soft on communism," Humphrey in 1954 leapfrogged the Republican position and proposed, by way of floor amendment, the outright abolition of the Communist party. This was not an instance of bidding up because the Democrats were almost certainly not trying to pass a ban on the communists, only to look as if they were. The Senate adopted Humphrey's amendment by a lopsided vote, but the amendment was not expected to become law since the Eisenhower administration strongly opposed it.

In previous elections Democrats had suffered from the "twenty years of treason" charge, and the communist issue was sure to arise again in the 1954 elections. The situation was particularly precarious because earlier that summer the Senate had voted to censure Senator

Joseph McCarthy, Republican of Wisconsin and arch foe of communism. Senators who voted to censure McCarthy stood some risk of being accused of abetting communism. Humphrey himself was a first-term senator up for reelection, and because of his liberal record was vulnerable to charges that he was soft on communism.

In August a bill concerning communist influence in labor unions came to the Senate floor. To labor supporters this was a union-busting bill, for it would authorize the United States attorney general and the Subversive Activities Control Board to deny unions deemed to be infiltrated by communists the right to engage in collective bargaining. Humphrey reportedly saw this bill as another instance of the Republicans using the communist threat to scare the public and win votes. He responded in kind.

On August 12 he offered his amendment, saying,

> I want Senators to stand up and answer whether they are for the Communist Party or against it.[28] I am tired of reading headlines about being 'soft' toward communism. I am tired of reading headlines about being a leftist, and about others being leftists. I am tired of people playing the Communist issue as though it were a great overture which has lasted for years. . . . This amendment will make the Communist Party, its membership, and its apparatus illegal. It would make membership in the Communist Party subject to criminal penalties. . . . I do not intend to be a half patriot. I will not be lukewarm. The issue is drawn.[29]

When asked whether they are for or against the Communist party, members of Congress must vote against, for otherwise someone will accuse them of being soft on communism. Humphrey's amendment passed eighty-four–zero on a roll-call vote. Voting to abolish the party was useful because it gave Democratic senators an unassailable position on communism. What more could one do to express one's antipathy toward communism? In the coming election, Democrats accused of being soft on communism could point out their vote to abolish the Communist party. After the vote a Democrat said: "Through the whole Congress Republicans cried 'Communist, Communist, Communist' against the Democrats and, though in control, did nothing about it. It was time to show them up and put them on the record. We called them and raised them and they fell into line like stampeding cattle."[30]

The genius of the amendment was that a ban was not likely to become law because it was opposed by the Eisenhower administration. The administration took the view that a ban would merely drive communists underground. Existing law required members of the Communist party to register with the government, making their activities easier to monitor. If membership in the party were illegal, the government could not require registration, for that would be self-incriminating and consequently in violation of the Fifth Amendment to the Constitution. This placed Republicans in the difficult position of defending a policy that made sense but could not readily be explained to the public. William Knowland accurately called the amendment a "Democratic tactical stunt [to] put Republicans in the position of protecting commies." With a sure Eisenhower veto awaiting the bill, Democratic senators whose scruples would normally prevent them from taking such a step could vote to outlaw a political party, knowing that no one's rights would be violated.

Needless to say, Eisenhower did not wish to be placed in the position of having to veto a bill outlawing the Communist party, and said that the Humphrey amendment opened the "darndest can of worms."[31] After adoption of the bill in the Senate, Eisenhower fought to keep the House from adopting a ban, which meant in practice keeping the House from even considering a ban (for if they considered it, they would pass it). Republicans devised a clever strategy to defuse the issue. A legislative leaders' meeting agreed that the House should adopt language that did not make the party illegal but merely concluded that "the CP should be outlawed."[32] This kept the Republicans from appearing to side with communists without undermining the Eisenhower administration's plans for fighting subversion. A participant in the meeting noted that the "word 'outlaw' doesn't mean anything in law," allowing Republicans to argue on the stump that they favored "outlawing" the Communist party, knowing that their bill had no force. Ultimately this plan was successful; the ban on the Communist party was deleted; in its modified form the bill was passed and signed by Eisenhower.[33]

Humphrey himself did not face a serious challenge to his reelection bid and probably did not benefit personally from his attempt to outlaw communism. But he claimed that the vote saved two Democratic Senate seats in the 1954 election.[34]

This is an instance of encroachment, not pursuit, because it is highly doubtful that Humphrey and his fellow Democrats were really trying to abolish the Communist party. Rather, they wanted to protect themselves from charges they were "soft" on communism. Considering Humphrey's otherwise sterling record as a liberal and advocate of civil liberties, it seems out of character for him to have supported a ban on a political party, unless he thought that ban would not become law. A hostile Humphrey biographer, seeking to demonstrate Humphrey's underhandedness, quotes him as having said elsewhere that "every state, every nation that has ever tried to outlaw a political party . . . has lived to rue the day."[35] Sponsoring the amendment was evidently good politics, but, Humphrey later commented, "It's not one of the things I'm proudest of."[36]

The Special Session of Congress in 1948

The Republican platform in 1948 was a form of strategic encroachment. Thomas E. Dewey, governor of New York and exemplar of progressive Republicanism, defeated Robert Taft of Ohio for the Republican presidential nomination. To satisfy its liberal presidential nominee, the convention endorsed a set of progressive positions on

Social Security, health care, housing, and so on. Samuel Rosenman, a speechwriter for FDR and Truman took "one look at Dewey's platform and pronounced it fit for any New Dealer to run on."[37] The decision of Dewey and Republican leaders to embrace liberal proposals must have reflected a judgment that the record of the Republican party, as expressed in the just completed Eightieth Congress, was too conservative for the average voter. They sought to indicate by word, but not deed, that the Republican party was in the mainstream of the country.

Dewey himself probably supported many, possibly all, of his platform's planks. But much of his party in Congress emphatically did not, and without congressional support Dewey would not be able to deliver on his platform if elected president. In this sense, then, the Republican platform represented a kind of political bait and switch—voters would be lured into the Republican store with promises of Dewey moderation, and walk out with Taft conservatism. While Dewey sought to blur the distinction between the parties, Truman's job was to keep Republicans from stealing Democratic issues and to highlight the distinction between the parties, and he sought to do this by focusing attention on the record of the "do-nothing" Eightieth Congress.

Conservatives felt betrayed by Dewey's platform, which made it hard for Dewey to pull off his maneuver. Republican congressional leaders were proud of the record of the Eightieth Congress and thought he should have run on it rather than distance himself from it. The Eightieth Congress, elected in 1946, was the first controlled by the Republicans since 1932, so Republican members of Congress had a lot of hard work before them in rolling back what they surely saw as fourteen years of Democratic mistakes and excesses. They did their best, passing Taft-Hartley, which limited the power of labor unions, and cutting taxes, over Truman vetoes. The Eightieth Congress also left a great deal of unfinished business.[38] Joe Martin wrote: "I cautioned him [Dewey] that he would be making a big mistake if he did not begin to talk about the constructive aspects of the Eightieth Congress and not let Truman get away, unanswered, with his constant criticism of it."[39] Charles Halleck, who was considered but rejected for the vice presidential nomination, claimed that if he had been on the ticket with Dewey, together they would have won because "he would never have allowed Dewey to sidestep the accomplishments of the Eightieth Congress."[40] Republican stalwart Phyllis Schlafly joined in conservative admiration for the Eightieth Congress, which, she said, "under the leadership of Robert Taft, had made the greatest record of any Congress in the 20th century."[41]

A perverse symmetry developed, with Truman and congressional conservatives in agreement that the record of the Eightieth Congress should be the focus of the presidential campaign. Dewey's judgment was that he should position himself near Truman, and through the platform sought to snuggle up close to Truman. On the other hand, Truman's problem was that the New Deal coalition that had elected Roosevelt four times had lost much of its energy, or, at least, that Truman had failed to energize it. One Democrat expressed the president's dilemma as follows: "Not that there is any hostility to Truman; rather, nobody seems to give a damn."[42] Clark Clifford devised a strategy for Truman to accentuate differences between himself and the Republican majority in Congress and to reestablish distance between himself and Dewey. A memo early in 1948 argued:

> The Administration should select the issues upon which there will be a conflict with the majority in Congress. It can assume it will get no major part of its program approved. Its tactics must, therefore, be entirely different than if there were any real point to bargaining and compromise. Its recommendations—in the State of the Union Message and elsewhere—must be tailored for the voter, not the Congressman; they must display a label which reads "no compromises."[43]

This part of the strategy worked exceedingly well as the Republicans cooperated by refusing to pass any major bills in 1948. Thus the distance between the Democratic and Republican parties was clarified and established. Next question: how to deal with Dewey's efforts to blur the distinction so carefully developed? By the time of the Democratic convention in the summer, Congress had adjourned for the year; Clifford and others urged the president to call a special session to allow the Republican majority in Congress to live up to the high ideals articulated in its platform. Another memo from Clifford argued for a special session:

> The boldest and most popular step the President could possibly take would be to call a special session of Congress in early August. This would: (1) focus attention on the rotten record of the Eightieth Congress, which the Republicans and the press will try to make the country forget; (2) force Dewey and [his running mate, Earl] Warren to defend the actions of Congress and make them accept Congress as a basic issue; (3) keep the steady glare of publicity on the Neanderthal men of the Republican party, who will embarrass Dewey and Warren.[44]

After the close of the Democratic convention, Truman called a special session of Congress, and asked for action on an eight-point program of legislation, including such issues as Social Security, public housing, the minimum wage, inflation controls, and civil rights.[45] All these were bills Truman had previously asked for and been denied by the Eightieth Congress, and most were now endorsed in some form in the Republican platform. It was, Joe Martin said, "a devilishly astute piece of politics."[46]

Truman's calculation was that Republicans in Congress would be unable or unwilling to pass any significant legislation, and that the exposure of Dewey's platform as hot air would confirm Republicans in the public mind as a party of reactionaries. Of course, sensible Republicans might conclude that their best defense would be a good offense, and that they should pass some of the legislation requested. Indeed, Herbert Brownell, Dewey's campaign manager, tried to persuade Republican leaders in Congress to pass some morsel of Truman's program in order to deflate the president's attacks.[47] In the Truman camp, Clark Clifford writes, "our greatest concern had been that they might pass two or three bills during the special session, and try to take the issue of a recalcitrant Congress away from us."[48] Truman and Clifford need not have worried, for it appears that Robert Taft's Ohio Republican uprightness left him unable to play political games. At a meeting of Brownell with Republican congressional leaders, Taft

> was adamant against acquiescing to Truman and none of the other leaders were willing to break with him on the issue. To Taft, a matter of principle was involved in Truman's political misuse of a Presidential prerogative; Brownell was appalled.
> . . . [Arthur] Vandenberg said, "Bob, I think we ought to do something. I think we ought to do whatever we can to show that we are trying to use the two weeks as best we can. Then we have a better case to take before the public." He proposed a couple of pieces of legislation which he thought should be passed, but Taft would not agree. [Hugh] Scott also urged some affirmative action; Taft ignored him. Vandenberg then suggested that they at least approve the International Wheat Agreement, arguing that it was a good measure and would help with the farm vote. "Bob Taft would have none of that," Scott relates. " 'No,' he said, 'we're not going to give that fellow anything.' Anyone familiar with Bob Taft's method of ending a conversation will know that was the end of it."[49]

Taft's high-mindedness (or stubbornness) played into Democratic strategy. The special session enacted a few minor measures but not enough to thwart Truman's plan of making the Eightieth Congress the focus of the campaign. He kept up his attacks, and prevented Dewey from disassociating himself from the Congress.[50]

The primary danger for Truman in calling the special session was that it could be seen as a partisan political ploy (which of course it was) and dismissed as such. But Truman was so far down compared to Dewey that dramatic action was called for; if it backfired, Truman would lose, but of course nearly everyone in the country thought he would lose anyway.[51] With nowhere to go but up, Truman used this blatantly political ploy. Republicans tried to call attention to the rank political character of the special session, but the judgment of contemporary observers was that Truman got the best of it, and he went on to win the election.

In cases of encroachment, no legislation passes because there was no possibility of an agreement. There was no strategic disagreement, only strategic agreement, an effort of one party to overcome the bargaining advantage of its opponent.

4   Provoking a Veto

I would remind you that extremism
in the defense of liberty is no vice!
And let me remind you also that moderation
in the pursuit of justice is no virtue!
—*Barry Goldwater*

The veto is an important source of presidential power,
and all modern presidents make use of this power, but
there is something of a puzzle as to why actual vetoes
should ever occur.[1] Presidents, after all, are seldom shy about telling
Congress what they want in legislation. Legislative leaders are good
vote counters, and as they work to pass a bill they should in most
instances know whether they will have enough votes to override a
veto. When they have the votes to override, they can disregard the
preferences and veto threats of the president, and pass the bill they
like. When they cannot override, they should pass a bill the president
will sign, if their goal is to have a law. The veto is a powerful tool,
but one that should remain largely unused, since good communication up and down Pennsylvania Avenue will allow Congress to anticipate presidential desires.[2] Despite the possibilities that exist for
working out disagreements in advance, vetoes occur regularly. This
chapter explores causes of vetoes and posits a new one: the deliberate
provocation of a veto by Congress, a form of strategic disagreement.

Some vetoes occur because of miscommunication between
branches of the government, such as when legislation proceeds
through Congress and the executive branch fails to make clear its
objections. This is most common in the case of minor legislation,

especially if it moves quickly late in a congressional session. After passage, the administration reviews the bill and, perhaps finding a fatal defect, vetoes it. Bills that fall victim to the pocket veto are often of this type.

Vetoes can also result from miscalculation or misunderstanding. Members of Congress may doubt a president's veto threat and pass a bill that does not conform to expressed requirements. In cases when the president has said he would veto any bill that does not satisfy specified criteria, Congress can pass a bill that the president will surely sign in order to avoid conflict and get the bill passed quickly. But members of Congress also recognize that vetoes are not costless to the president, and that he may sign a bill that is not ideal in order to avoid the conflict associated with the veto and override attempt. Therefore it may be worthwhile to chance a veto in the hope that even if the president does not like the bill in all respects, he will sign it. Presidents may also conclude that the bill passed by Congress is superior to the status quo and sign it despite imperfections.

Vetoes resulting from miscalculation and miscommunication are largely accidental, the product of uncertainty about the president's preferences or intentions.

This chapter explores a source of vetoes that has not been examined previously: the deliberate provocation of a veto by Congress in order to generate political advantages for members of Congress and harm for the president. This occurs exclusively under divided party government. When the party controlling Congress has an advantage over the president, it can be a useful strategy for Congress to pass an uncompromising bill that the president vigorously opposes to curry favor with an important constituency and generate a presidential veto. This important and attractive tactic accentuates differences between parties and provides information about the parties' positions. If by chance the president signs the bill into law, the lines dividing the parties are blurred, but the party in Congress gets exactly the policy it wants.

Despite its benefits, the veto strategy is not always desirable or feasible. For one thing, it is usable only under divided party government; seldom does Congress want to embarrass a president of the same party in this way. It can also be difficult to get Congress to pass legislation guaranteed to provoke a veto.

Practitioners seldom if ever confess their purpose, but there are several circumstantial indications that a veto was not accidental, but provoked. Vetoes are "provoked" when members of Congress pass a bill they expect and want the president to veto because they will obtain political benefits. When a bill draws votes largely or entirely from the majority party, wins with less than a two-thirds majority, and is passed despite a promised presidential veto, we can surmise that the point of passing the bill was not to make a law but to harm the president and satisfy interested constituencies.[3] The president is almost sure to veto the bill and Congress will not be able to override. Such bills can be termed "veto bait."

The passage of veto bait is a regular feature of divided party government. In 1975 and 1976 Congress, controlled by the Democrats, challenged President Ford by passing a series of bills they knew he would veto, presumably to force him to veto the bill and attract the enmity of whatever group favored the bill. Two apparent cases of veto bait were an emergency housing bill and Hatch Act revisions. The housing bill—H.R. 4485—was intended to boost employment in the construction industry and make housing more affordable. Ford objected on the grounds that the assistance would come too late to have an effect on the current recession, and that the distribution of benefits would be regressive. Despite unambiguous veto threats from Ford, the House passed the bill 253–155 and the Senate passed it 72–24. Republican majorities opposed the bill in both chambers. To no one's surprise, Ford vetoed the bill. The story of the Hatch Act revision is nearly the same. If adopted, the bill would

have loosened restrictions on the political activities of federal workers. Republicans objected that the bill would politicize the bureau-
cracy. First the House passed the bill—H.R. 8617—by a vote of
241–146. Ford said he would veto the bill unless modified. The Senate acted next, and did not succumb to the threat, passing the bill in
nearly identical form, 54–36. When it was sent to the president, he
vetoed it. In both cases the vetoes were sustained, and indeed proponents of these bills never had a realistic expectation that they would
be able to override, since both bills passed with less than a two-thirds
majority in at least one chamber. But the Democrats persisted in
passing the housing bill to please the construction industry, and
passed the Hatch Act revision to satisfy federal workers. Both were
constituencies from which the Democrats needed and wanted support.

Family and medical leave legislation under President Bush also
qualifies ideally as veto bait. President Bush said he supported the
idea of family leave, but believed it should be negotiated between
workers and employers, and not imposed by government requirements. The House passed its bill 259–157, with only thirty-nine Republicans voting "yea." Senate Republicans, aware of the president's
veto threat, saw little need to go on the record, so the bill passed
without a recorded vote in the Senate. Bush vetoed the bill as expected, and the override attempt in the House failed. Senator Chris-
topher Dodd declared that "George Bush is going to have a family
leave bill on his desk every year that he's in office."[4] The point was
not to pass the bill, but to make Bush pay a price with women voters
for his resistance, to make clear to women voters that Democrats
were on their side, and to help mobilize supporters for the next election.

Several times under Presidents Bush and Reagan Congress passed
trade legislation that increased the level of protection for the domestic textile industry. These bills were understood to have no chance
of becoming law because both presidents were vigorous, outspoken

defenders of free trade. But Democrats persisted in passing them, often right before an election, no doubt because communicating to predominantly southern textile workers that Democrats, not Republicans, looked out for their interests was a way of helping Democratic candidates in some important congressional elections.[5]

These bills were veto bait, passed by Congress with little or no expectation that they would become law. Had Democrats in Congress really wanted to pass these bills, they would have engaged in negotiations with the Republicans to overcome presidential objections, or at least to produce veto-proof two-thirds majorities in both chambers of Congress. They must have known and expected that bills passed on a partisan basis would be vetoed, and they preferred dead, uncompromising bills to compromise laws.

Congressional Strategies

Passing veto bait is frequently difficult, which limits the usefulness of the veto strategy. By its nature, veto bait is controversial legislation and Congress, because of its complex legislative process, is far better at killing than at passing controversial bills. Most important bills pass by large margins under both unified and divided government because congressional procedure favors consensual legislation.[6] Because Republicans are unlikely to cooperate with Democrats in an effort to pass a bill to embarrass a Republican president,[7] the Democrats have to get nearly all votes from their own party to pass the bill, often a great challenge. If a committee with jurisdiction, or the chair of a committee or subcommittee is uncooperative, the effort to pass veto bait can stall. In the Senate, the strenuous objection of even one member willing to object to unanimous consent requests or to filibuster can block enactment of a bill, so if the president has allies in the Senate willing to go all out, the veto bait can usually be blocked.

In the summer of 1992, Democrats in Congress tried to give the presidential campaign of Bill Clinton a boost by provoking a veto of a bill favoring abortion rights. This plan was bungled when the

Democrats could not get the bill out of Congress, sparing President Bush the necessity of vetoing it, as he surely would have.[8] Merely passing the bill in one chamber or offering an amendment on the floor can be modestly helpful in marking the relative party positions, but it does not provide the compelling drama of congressional passage followed by a veto.

The veto strategy is most attractive shortly before an election, when it can have the greatest electoral impact, and when there may soon be a change in government that allows Congress to pass exactly the bill it prefers.[9] If the election is distant, voters may fail to remember on election day the measures taken on their behalf. Moreover, a longer interval before the next election means that waiting for a more favorable administration to assume office is less attractive. The approach of an election and the end of the Congress not only increase the value of the veto strategy but make it harder to use. At the end of each Congress, the crush of legislative business rises as representatives strive to get their pet bills enacted before the end of the session kills all pending legislation. Passing veto bait provides political benefits, but devoting time to bills that never become law leaves less time for other bills that could become law. Legislators keen on passing a particular bill may see the veto strategy as a waste of time and an impediment to passing their favorite bill.

A variation on the veto strategy is for Congress first to pass an uncompromising bill that the president vetoes, and then to pass a scaled-back version that the president will sign. We can call this tactic "successive approximation." The game can actually be played out over several iterations with Congress moving gradually toward the point where the president will sign a bill. Successive approximation accomplishes two purposes. It allocates credit and blame relatively clearly, indicating that the majority in Congress tried their best to enact the ideal bill favored by constituency groups, and that the president vetoed it. But by coming back with a second (or third) bill that becomes law, the Democrats get benefits for their constituents. This is probably as close as they can come to having both a bill and an issue. But because the president does finally sign the bill, and can take some credit for it, responsibility is necessarily more ambiguous than when no bill is passed after a veto.

Successive approximation also helps deal with uncertainty concerning the president's position. Presidential threats to veto a bill could be bluffs, intended to persuade the Congress to pass a modest bill. By passing a pure form of the bill first, Congress can test the president's veto threat and give the group in question a chance to lobby the president. If Congress caves into the veto threat and passes the more limited bill first, it could be settling for less than it might get.

In a contest over a housing bill in 1959 Democrats appear to have employed successive approximation. The Democratic Congress passed a housing construction bill. Eisenhower called it "extravagant" and vetoed it. Congress passed a second bill, scaled down some but still not conforming exactly to Eisenhower's specifications; he vetoed it too. A third bill, making further concessions, was passed and signed.[10]

In 1989 Congress pursued this tactic with minimum wage legislation, first passing a bill that President Bush found objectionable, and which he vetoed, and then passing a bill he would sign. President Bush indicated early in the process that he would veto any increase in the minimum wage above $4.25 an hour. In addition, he insisted that any increase in the minimum wage be accompanied by a "training wage" provision whereby employers could hire new workers and pay them less than the minimum wage for a specified period of time. The original Democratic bill ignored both of these demands, calling for a $4.56 an hour minimum without any training wage. As the bill moved through Congress the wage fell by ten cents and a training wage was introduced, albeit with a shorter duration than Bush preferred. Thirty cents an hour and disagreements over the training wage still separated the two sides when the bill cleared Congress.

The amount of money on the line may not have been great, but the stakes were quite high, for President Bush had vetoed no legislation before this, and if he backed down now his credibility would be damaged. Congress then delayed sending the bill to the president for a month to give the AFL-CIO and other groups time to mobilize support for the legislation. The Democratic strategy was both to test the president and to make him pay as much as possible should he the veto the bill, which he did. An override effort failed.

Then came the question of what to do next. The first plan was to send Bush a series of bills that moved incrementally toward the $4.25 demanded, forcing him to choose between repeatedly vetoing a bill to help the poorest workers (and middle-class teenagers working at fast food restaurants) and breaking his pledge not to sign a bill giving more than $4.25 an hour. But the Democrats reconsidered. The public response to the President's veto was distinctly muted, and it was likely that rather than boost their political position, provoking additional vetoes would primarily highlight their inability to override. Pressure to compromise was also felt by Republicans in Congress, who wanted to get the minimum wage behind them so they could press for a capital gains tax cut without projecting the appearance that Republicans sought to help only the rich.[11] Therefore, the Democrats in Congress passed a new bill that accepted the $4.25-an-hour minimum wage and incorporated only a very limited training wage. With the president backing down on the training wage and the Democrats giving ground on the minimum wage, it was a compromise that left both sides reasonably satisfied. Bush could tell conservatives he had stood firm against the liberals, and the liberals could say they had tried their best, and that, by provoking a confrontation, had even managed to extract concessions from the president.

The strategy of successive approximation cannot be used on bills that are extremely difficult and time consuming to get through Congress. The cost of the veto to Congress is relatively high, because passing the bill the second time will probably absorb much scarce floor time in Congress. There was some question of whether President Bush would have vetoed the Clean Air Bill in 1990 if Congress had not trimmed the bill in several places. But clean air legislation was so hard to get out of Congress at all that its supporters could not risk a veto, because they might not have been able to pass another bill anytime soon. Nor can the strategy be used at the end of the session, because there may not be time to pass another bill.

A sure veto from the president can, ironically, make it easier for Congress to engage in veto strategies. When a bill has a substantial chance of becoming law, Congress must "sweat" the details and resolve lingering, difficult controversies. This both increases the time needed to pass a bill and reduces the probability of its passing. But if a presidential veto is certain, Congress can leave controversies unresolved. With Republicans in the White House, Democrats in Congress passed campaign finance reform bills that called for limits on congressional campaign spending and public finance, two policies that were anathema to Republicans, ensuring a presidential veto. This made the bill easier to pass because the Democrats did not have to fight over the treatment of "soft money," an important issue that divided the party.[12]

Presidential Strategies

When the president vetoes a bill he incurs some cost, the magnitude of which is determined both by the outrage of the group deprived and by the importance of that group to the president and his party.[13] If the group that benefits from the bill is unlikely to vote for the president under any circumstances, the cost of the veto is low. The cost of offending swing groups is higher. The president's popularity may also affect veto behavior: an extremely popular president may be more inclined than an unpopular one to take on a group by vetoing its bill. Presidents can also see some vetoes as beneficial, especially if they can use the veto to claim they are standing up to special interests and big spenders.

Whether it actually hurts a president to veto legislation is an important question beyond the scope of this study. For purposes here, it is sufficient that both legislative and executive branches act as if vetoes were costly. Congress provokes them and presidents often try to avoid vetoes of popular bills. If they veto legislation, they try to devise explanations that make the best of the situation. Presidents Ford and Bush both made ample use of the veto, and, in efforts to make the best of the situation, portrayed themselves as principled defenders of the country against profligate Congresses. Both faced Congresses with large Democratic majorities that were intent on making a record.[14]

When the president does not want to be forced to veto a bill, the first line of defense is to stop the bill's enactment, a strategy that requires the close cooperation of the president's supporters in Congress. In 1960, as Congress was getting ready to consider a bill providing federal aid to education, Vice President Nixon asserted that "a bill on the president's desk that he could not approve would be the worst possible situation," for it would require a veto and presumably help Democrats in the election.[15] To avoid a veto, the president's supporters in Congress must modify the bill enough to allow the president to sign it, or, if that is unsuccessful, scuttle it altogether. When the task is that of killing a popular bill and obscuring responsibility so that no one can be blamed, Congress is far better than the president. A presidential veto is an extraordinarily public event, whereas the complex procedure of Congress allows bills to be killed, wounded, or merely delayed in many ways that cannot be easily explained to the outsider. Senators have the special privilege of being able to filibuster to keep a bill they oppose from being passed. Unfortunately, the filibuster affords no anonymity.

If the president is concerned about the adverse political consequences of vetoing a bill on a sensitive issue, it may also be that members of his party in Congress do not want to vote against it either, and may even be eager for an opportunity to show their support. In these cases both the president and his party in Congress will want the bill to die, but neither will want to deliver the death blow. Of course, the president may conclude that, if he cannot persuade his supporters in Congress to vote against the bill on original passage, perhaps he should sign the bill because Congress will probably vote for an override later, ensuring its success and making the president's veto a futile gesture. Presidents Reagan and Bush differed on this point. Reagan was overridden more often than Bush because he vetoed more bills that Congress had passed overwhelmingly.

When a bill is overwhelmingly popular, the president is likely to sign it. But he will sometimes be compelled to veto popular legislation, especially when doing otherwise would alienate important supporters. Nixon signed a 20 percent increase in Social Security despite serious reservations, primarily because nearly everyone in Congress had supported it and his advisers considered a veto very politically damaging. Given the widespread recognition that the Social Security increase was unstoppable, a presidential signature could not have been very damaging to Nixon, even among the most conservative elements (provided they realized that the bill would become law with or without Nixon's signature). But if a veto is perceived as less than suicidal, a president may veto the bill even when it is quite popular. The reasons are coalition maintenance and ideology. Each party represents a more or less loose coalition of interests and beliefs (Democrats more loose, Republicans less so), and each party tries to avoid taking positions that will alienate important bases of support. After Congress passed family leave legislation, which embodied an idea popular with women voters, Bush may have felt tempted to sign it, but did not because it so violated notions of free enterprise the administration cherished that signing the bill would have ruptured ties with some of the administration's core supporters.

If they cannot prevent the enactment of obnoxious bills, presidents veto those they must and try to make the best of it. They seek to turn the legislation against Congress by emphasizing its cost, its impact on jobs, or whatever will serve their case the best. Republican presidents hounded by partisan, aggressive Democratic Congresses (in particular, Ford and Bush) have been forced by circumstances to veto large numbers of bills that were popular with important constituencies. Bush vetoed civil rights legislation, a minimum wage bill, a family leave bill, and so on. Ford vetoed, among others, an emergency jobs bill on the eve of an election. Both presidents defended themselves by portraying Democrats in Congress as irresponsible and profligate, and themselves as sober defenders of the economy, jobs, and the rights of citizens. Faced with the Republican Eightieth Congress, Harry Truman made frequent use of the veto and, in the case of Taft-Hartley, his advisers considered it most beneficial, "enhancing Truman's image as defender of the common man. . . . [Chester] Bowles predicted that even if the veto were overridden [which it was], the Democrats would gain a 'clear political advantage.' "[16]

When the president is forced by circumstances to sign a popular but distasteful bill, he does all he can to gather credit for himself and members of his party, and exclude his tormentors. The bill-signing ceremony is one way, controlled entirely by the president, to apportion credit. For the signing of important legislation, the president invites television reporters and their cameras to the White House (or other locations likely to communicate an appropriate message) to watch him sign the bill and give a speech praising its goals and associating himself with its purposes. Presidents can try to take credit for legislation they sign, regardless of their position on the bill as it worked its way through Congress. In 1990 President Bush was said to be interested in signing the Clean Air Act in California, to prove to environmentally conscious Californians immediately before the midterm election that he was an "environmental president," and to share some of his presidential aura with a Republican candidate in a close race for governor. Both the House and Senate had approved the conference report on the Clean Air bill ten days before the election, but to prevent the president from stealing credit for the bill and using it to help Republican candidates, Democrats in Congress deliberately delayed enrollment of the bill and did not send it to the president for his signature until after the election. In return, President Bush signed the Clean Air Act in a ceremony that deliberately excluded all the Democrats who had made it possible.[17] When President Nixon signed the Clean Air Act of 1970 he pointedly did not invite Senator Edmund Muskie, the principle mover of the bill, because Muskie was both a Democrat and a leading candidate for the White House.

Provoking a veto is a form of strategic disagreement whereby the majority party in Congress passes a bill despite the expectation of a presidential veto, because it expects the veto to help their party and hurt the president. In some cases the choice of this tactic will keep a signable bill from being enacted. In other cases there will have been no chance of passing a bill that the president would sign, and in these instances veto provocation is primarily to remind interested constituencies of the differences between the parties.

5 Stalemates and Summit Negotiations

The best is the
enemy of the good.
—*Voltaire*

When two sets of politicians compete for a single constituency, they are likely to engage in a game of pursuit and avoidance, as depicted in previous chapters. When two sets of politicians seek to appeal to distinctly different constituencies and offer divergent policy prescriptions, they are unlikely to chase after each other. Instead we should expect a stalemate: no movement, and perhaps even no bargaining. The possibility of joint gains forms the basis for negotiations, and where the purposes of the parties are entirely opposed, negotiations seem pointless.

This chapter examines bargaining in cases where (1) legislation must pass to prevent a calamity, (2) its enactment requires adopting measures very unpopular with valued constituencies, such as increasing taxes and cutting program benefits, and (3) no one party or faction can unilaterally pass a bill that imposes costs on its opponents, making compromise in which all sides accept distasteful measures the only way to resolve the dispute. Reaching an agreement is exceedingly difficult in these cases, but also most important. In such cases, negotiators may well consider the unthinkable, such as inflicting harm upon their most valued constituencies, but not before exhausting other alternatives. A stalemate is very likely to develop as the parties feel each other out, hoping the other will capitulate. They may delay just to put off something they find unpleasant. Unusual bargaining patterns emerge as well, with the bargainers sometimes actually moving apart, adopting more extreme positions, rather than moderating and moving closer together.

When the two parties to a negotiation prefer completely different solutions to a problem, the disagreement most often will be neither contrived nor strategic, but genuine. Yet the cases considered in this chapter involve strategic disagreement on both sides, a form of mutual avoidance. The tactics considered here count as strategic disagreement because all through the protracted negotiations, there was a possible compromise agreement that would make both Democrats and Republicans better off than they would be with no bill at all. Both sides avoided the agreement because they were reluctant to alienate constituents or sacrifice political advantages over their opponents, and also because they were concerned about the hazards of making a reasonable proposal.

The normal political bargaining process, characterized by the public, sequential exchange of offers, discourages the emergence of controversial agreements. Politicians are never eager to make proposals that offend their supporters, but they are further deterred from submitting sensible, reasonable offers because of uncertainty about the response from the other side. Politicians who make "reasonable" offers (those that could lead to an agreement because they impose costs in a balanced manner) can easily find themselves attacked by both their friends and enemies, and to avoid that unpleasant fate they propose instead "unreasonable" offers, self-serving solutions that impose all costs on the other side, and which have no chance of being adopted. Such proposals do have the virtue of not alienating key supporters. In response, sponsors of these proposals are attacked by their enemies, but they are used to that and typically can give as good as they get. None of this helps to solve a problem or promote necessary compromise. All is not hopeless, however. The use of summit negotiations offers real promise as a means of reaching agreements because they allow the bargainers to arrive at an accord behind closed doors and eliminate the uncertainty of making an offer in public. This chapter examines the problems of public, sequential bargaining, and uses two cases of stalemate to show how they develop and how, under the right conditions, summit negotiations can help encourage resolution.

In 1983, the Social Security system went to the brink of insolvency while Congress and the president blamed each other for its demise. Democrats who early on had proposed moderate, balanced solutions to the problem of Social Security financing took increasingly extreme positions later. President Reagan proposed a completely one-sided solution to the problem, based exclusively on benefit reductions, and got it with both barrels from Democrats and defenders of Social Security. Thereafter Republicans, put on the defensive by Democratic attacks, said nothing whatsoever.

In 1987, a sequestration order under Gramm-Rudman was very nearly implemented. Instead of taking action to prevent this occurrence, Democrats and Republicans consoled themselves with the knowledge that they could blame each other for the mindless consequences of sequestration. Democrats proposed tax increases as a means of cutting the deficit while President Reagan and other Republicans denounced them repeatedly and severely, vowing to veto any tax increase, despite having previously proposed a variety of tax increases.

In both cases, political stalemate nearly led to disaster. In both, resolution of the problem at hand was made either much harder or impossible by the efforts of the two parties to extract partisan political advantage from the situation. And in both, the problem was ultimately resolved by means of direct, bipartisan negotiations between the parties and between the legislative and executive branches of government.

In the cases of both Social Security and deficit reduction, the problem was how to distribute a very large cost between the two sides. This was a zero-sum conflict, in that an agreement that was better for one side was necessarily worse for the other. Yet as Paul Quirk observes, the budget deficit is a case of mixed motive bargaining, where an agreement does provide mutual gains that help offset the costs incurred. The same was true of Social Security rescue legislation.[1] In return for adopting unpopular legislation, the deficit can be reduced and solvency of Social Security assured. But the blessings of deficit reduction figure far less prominently in the political calculations of both Democrats and Republicans than the defense of programs that the parties "own."[2] Through the Reagan and Bush years, neither party exhibited much enthusiasm for deficit reduction, but both showed great zeal in defense of their programs and properties. Roger Fisher and William Ury stress the usefulness of negotiators striving to create new options that reduce direct conflict and produce mutual gains. This can be done, they assert, by extending one-dimensional problems into additional dimensions.[3] Fisher and Ury exhort negotiators to "look for items that are of low cost to you and high benefit to them, and vice versa. Differences in interests, priorities, beliefs, forecasts, and attitudes toward risk all make dovetailing possible."[4] Where such dovetailing can be found, conflicts can be muted and otherwise difficult bargaining eased. Despite such optimistic prescriptions, there remain obdurate cases without significant dovetailing, where reaching an agreement requires both sides to make painful concessions.

Both Social Security rescue and deficit reduction present difficult bargaining situations because the potential gains—smaller deficits and the continued solvency of Social Security—are pure public goods that benefit both sides equally. Moreover, while the gains are real they are somewhat distant from the lives of ordinary voters. The benefit is prospective, the avoidance of a future harm, but it must be paid for today from money in hand. In both cases, the contending parties must "buy" deficit reduction or Social Security rescue with concessions in other programs they value, and their constituents value the benefit being purchased less, perhaps irrationally so, than the sacrifice needed to buy it.[5]

The Obviousness of the Solution

The one great aid to reaching an agreement in these cases was a highly structured, symmetrical bargaining situation that strongly suggested from the very start that any negotiated agreement would reflect the same symmetry. Common sense and theories of bargaining both indicate that the only possible way to achieve an agreement in such cases is through some sort of balanced compromise. And in fact, after months of public haggling and briefer periods of private negotiations, the result in both of these cases was an agreement that, in its general outline, could have been predicted well in advance.

In general, for the Social Security and budget issues, bargaining between Congress and a president with divided party control of the government could be characterized in the following manner:

1. The two sides both wanted a solution but preferred almost completely different means. In both cases, Republicans preferred spending cuts while Democrats preferred revenue increases. This is a simplification of the preferences of the parties, since there is diversity in both parties. But the dominant factions of the parties are as characterized.

2. For an agreement to be implemented, the consent of both president and Congress was necessary. Congress was extremely unlikely to override a veto, which meant that the Democrats could not force a Democratic plan on the president. Since legislation was required, the president could not unilaterally implement a solution through an executive order or other administrative action.

3. The failure to agree would hurt both the president and Congress, Democrats and Republicans, about equally. The collapse of Social Security would be a disaster of nearly unimaginable proportions for which the public would probably fail to discriminate be-

tween the two parties in their desire to visit revenge upon politicians. Consequently, it is reasonable to believe that both sides would suffer enormously, and similarly. Failure to avoid budgetary sequestration in 1987 would have had less certain consequences, but since the budget deficit was blamed for the November 1987 stock market crash, it was widely thought possible that failure to avoid sequestration might have caused further, worse declines of the stock market. Had an economic disaster resulted from a failure of the government to reach a compromise, both Democrats and Republicans could have expected to share the blame.

4. Uncertainty over each other's bargaining positions was minimal. Democrats normally have a good understanding of the political constraints on the Republicans, and vice versa. Democrats know that Republicans hate to increase taxes, while Republicans know that Democrats hate to cut programs. These aversions are well understood on both sides, limiting the opportunity for one side to misrepresent its bargaining position in order to gain an advantage. Of course this does not prevent negotiators from trying to misrepresent their position for strategic gain. If one side could somehow make a plausible case that, for example, a dollar's worth of spending cuts are as politically painful for the Democrats as two dollars of tax increases are to the Republicans, that might enhance its bargaining position. Similarly, parties can engage in efforts to "commit" themselves irrevocably to a position as a way of ruling out certain kinds of concessions, thereby strengthening their position.[6] One may reasonably interpret George Bush's "no new taxes" pledge as not only a means of getting elected, but also as a way of making it costly to back down later. Of course it was not successful, for he backed down and paid a great price.

These conditions imply a highly symmetrical relationship between the branches of government, in which neither side has power or bargaining advantage over the other. It so happens that these conditions are very close to those imposed by John Nash in his classic article "The Bargaining Problem." Nash assumes that "the two individuals are highly rational, that each can accurately compare his desires for various things, that they are equal in bargaining skill, and that each has full knowledge of the tastes and preferences of the other."[7] The implication of Nash's solution to such games is that, where both sides stand to benefit equally from an agreement (or to lose equally in the event of a failure to agree), the two sides should meet each other halfway. Howard Raiffa also cites experimental evidence that in highly symmetric bargaining games, where the two sides know each other's preferences, there is a strong tendency to settle upon the fifty-fifty division.[8]

Where the two sides are not symmetric in bargaining strength, we should expect some corresponding difference in the agreement. When one side can credibly contend that it cannot make an equal sacrifice, that side enjoys a substantial bargaining advantage. Thomas Schelling discusses this point at substantial length and with great insight in *The Strategy of Conflict*.[9] In the 1987 budget negotiations, which produced the less equal solution of the two cases studied here, the Democrats' position was strengthened because, first, domestic spending had already taken the brunt of spending cuts in previous years, while taxes had been cut and defense spending increased; and second, despite the president's insistence on large domestic cuts, support for that policy did not exist in either party in Congress. Consequently, an equal division did not occur, and the president was forced to make greater concessions.

Game theory aside, sensible people need no fancy apparatus to understand intuitively that, where neither side has the power to compel the other, and where both sides lose similarly from the failure to agree, neither can demand that the other make a grossly disproportionate sacrifice. Politicians are sophisticated players of the political game. Democrats certainly know that Republicans will not accept a deal that injures Republican political interests but not Democratic interests, and vice versa. Knowing this did not prevent politicians from making offers that were grossly one-sided in both cases. But after all was said and done, the final agreements were fairly close to what game theory and common sense suggested they should be—a balanced compromise.

The Problem of Explaining Compromise

The politicians who negotiate agreements understand that compromise is inevitable in politics. But they have a hard time communicating this necessity to constituents, and thus are often reluctant to enter into a compromise. A politician can avoid the messiness of explaining a controversial decision by never taking a position that cannot readily be explained to constituents or voting in a way that offers an opening for a potential opponent or rival.[10] The prudent course of action is never to agree to any compromise that harms one's constituents.

The ordeal of a politician who wants to compromise is compounded by the presence of rivals for the loyalty of a group, who undermine efforts to explain controversial decisions by asserting that compromise was not necessary. In the case of the Social Security rescue of 1983, the leaders of advocacy groups for the elderly attacked the summit agreement, arguing that there should have been no benefit cuts. Educating the public is very difficult when the public receives conflicting messages.

Negotiations that take place as a part of a political contest between two parties can be extremely difficult to conclude successfully, because the actions calculated to generate constituency loyalty tend to undermine negotiations, and vice versa. A willingness to compromise and to eschew strident language encourages success in negotiations. However, bargaining away something valued by a constituency threatens the support and trust of that constituency. The fact that such compromises must be made in order to reach agreement does not mollify a deprived and enraged constituency. To a very large extent, parties to negotiations must decide whether to seek partisan advantage or to make good public policy. And they will choose to make good public policy rather than seek partisan advantage only when they must do so to avert disaster, and even then only at the last possible moment.

Problems of Sequential, Public Bargaining

The sequential nature of normal, public executive-legislative bargaining impedes the search for an agreement. The government typically responds to a perceived problem in sequential fashion, with either the president (or his minions), a congressional committee, or an informal set of like-minded legislators initiating the process by offering a proposal. This they do by issuing a report, holding a press conference, introducing legislation, giving a speech, or some combination of the above. The initial proposal elicits responses and counterproposals from other interested elites, among them the president (if the proposal emerged from Congress), members of Congress, and interest group leaders. They indicate approbation or disgust, suggest changes, express reservations, denounce the entire enterprise as misguided or demented, and so on. Commonly, when the president issues a proposal, his opponents in Congress will follow that with a counterproposal (or vice versa), and the counterproposal will elicit an equivalent set of responses from interested observers.

The process of making proposals and responding to them is a kind of negotiation, undertaken by elites with other elites as the audience, but it is done in full public view, and the proposals and offers are designed to appeal both to the mass audience and to elite bargainers. Proposals ostensibly directed at other elites can have as their real purpose the goal of gaining or retaining the support of voters and constituencies, or of embarrassing the other side. Indeed, one side may respond to another's offer with an excoriating blast intended not to advance negotiations but to play to constituent opinion. It can also respond more moderately, indicating a desire for serious discussions. Uncertainty about the intentions of one's partner—specifically, about whether it is the partner's intention to bargain in good faith or to bash the opponent—reduces the likelihood that either side will engage in serious negotiations.

In framing an offer, the president or Congress has a choice between making a "reasonable" or an "unreasonable" offer.[11] A reasonable offer imposes costs on both sides in roughly similar proportions, while an unreasonable offer imposes nearly all costs on the other side. A reasonable offer is intended to lead to negotiations and an agreement. It indicates that its proposer is interested in reaching an agreement, not in posturing for constituents or attacking the opponent. An unreasonable offer is intended to appeal to one's constituencies and will be rejected immediately by the other side because of its inherent unfairness. It is unreasonable because its authors know it cannot be adopted, and its purpose is not to move toward agreement but to appeal to constituents. The primary audience for reasonable offers is other elites, while the audience for unreasonable offers is interest groups and constituents.

Reasonable offers are attended by risks and benefits. The risk is that, in making a reasonable offer, one demonstrates a willingness to compromise, which may be interpreted by some supporters as a failure to support their interests with sufficient enthusiasm. Rival politicians within a party and interest group leaders may endorse this interpretation and attack the author of a reasonable proposal in an effort to attract support. The benefit of reasonableness is that it may lead ultimately to an agreement. If politicians could be certain that making a reasonable offer would in fact lead to an agreement, they would be far more inclined to accept the risks.

When a reasonable offer has been proposed, the other side can respond by making a reasonable counterproposal or going on the attack. A reasonable counterproposal welcomes the constructive attitude of the opponent, and increases the likelihood that the two sides will be able to make progress toward an agreement. A reasonable counterproposal carries with it many of the same risks as a reasonable proposal: it indicates a willingness to betray one's own supporters and presents rivals within one's party with an opportunity for criticism. Rather than incur such a risk one can use the occasion of the reasonable offer as an opportunity to launch an attack on the opponent, refusing to consider any concession that would hurt one's own constituents. This does nothing to help produce an agreement, but it does make constituencies happy and deprives rivals of an issue.

If a reasonable offer is met by an attack, the party making the offer loses doubly. First, the problem is no closer to being solved, and second, the party making the offer has indicated to possibly loyal supporters that it is willing to sacrifice their interests. The responding party loses nothing and gains something. It has done nothing to alienate its constituents while the other side has. Unless a party knows in advance how the other side will respond, it is probably unwise to make a reasonable offer. But given the nature of the negotiating process, it is difficult to know in advance how the other side will respond.

If the offer is unreasonable, the choice of how to respond is simple—denounce the proposal and its authors. When a party has made it clear that it is most interested in cultivating its constituency, putting forth a balanced counterproposal makes no sense. The other side would only use it as an opportunity for a new attack.

Figure 5.1, which represents this process of offer and counteroffer by means of a decision tree (in which the president is depicted as the first mover), reveals several elements of this strategic process. First, regardless of one's intentions, it is better to go second than first. If one intends to cooperate, it is better to wait for the other party to make an offer and show its intentions. If one's intention is to defect, it is also better to go second, hoping that the opponent will walk into a trap by making a reasonable offer. Nothing can be lost by going second! Furthermore, there is always less risk in being unreasonable. If one does go first, there is little sense in making a reasonable offer, for it offers the other side a target that may be too attractive to resist. If against all odds a reasonable offer should be made, the second mover probably should defect. Cooperating helps to produce an agreement, which benefits both sides equally. Defecting hurts the other side and benefits one's own side. Therefore, defecting is preferable. It does not help solve the problem, but there is always tomorrow.

The Development of Political Stalemate: Social Security
The politics of the Social Security rescue and of the 1987 budget agreement exemplify the problems of dealing with contentious issues under divided government. In both cases serious negotiations and reasonable proposals were abandoned as partisanship escalated.

Figure 5.1
Decision Tree of Interbranch, Sequential, Public Negotiations

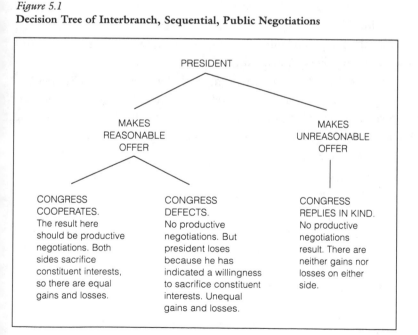

In 1980 it became apparent that the old-age portion of the Social Security system was heading toward financial troubles. Consequently, the Social Security subcommittee of the House Ways and Means Committee began to write legislation to put the system on a sound financial base. In early 1981 Representative J. J. Pickle (D-Tex.), who chaired that subcommittee, prepared legislation that relied on an infusion of general revenues to get over a short-term problem:[12] some tax increases and some benefit cuts, in particular, a deferred, gradual increase in the Normal Retirement Age. This legislation was proceeding through the subcommittee, where it enjoyed bipartisan support.[13]

At this point the Reagan administration entered the picture. Although it was interested in keeping Social Security solvent, it also wished to reduce the overall federal deficit, which by the spring and summer of 1981 had become a problem of major proportions. From the standpoint of deficit reductions, the subcommittee bill was horrendous. The bulk of its spending reductions would take place well after the Reagan administration had vacated the White House. And because it relied on general revenues, it would actually increase the budget deficit for some time. Office of Management and Budget Director David Stockman's reaction was extremely negative. "The moment I heard about the contents of the Pickle bill," he recalls, "I was determined to derail it."[14] Administration officials requested that the subcommittee temporarily suspend its activity to give the Social Security Administration an opportunity to produce a plan. After receiving the president's approval, this plan was unveiled on May 12, 1981.

The administration's proposals consisted entirely of benefit reductions. If implemented, the proposals would not only solve all problems of Social Security financing, but, because they would reduce Social Security spending by twice the amount needed to ensure solvency, they would also help to reduce the rest of the federal deficit. This seemed to many observers less a Social Security rescue than a clear effort to milk Social Security for budget savings to offset administration-backed tax cuts.

The reaction was immediate and harsh. Although many proposals were reasonable, the administration's plan ran into serious and widespread public opposition because of the suddenness with which some aspects were to take effect. The most damaging aspect of the package was the immediate reduction of benefits for persons taking early-retirement benefits at ages sixty-two to sixty-four.[15] If the proposal was enacted, this meant that people retiring with the expectation of a certain level of Social Security benefit would receive a lower benefit.

The Democrats sensed an outstanding political opportunity and they exploited it magnificently. Just days before, on May 8, the Democrats had taken a beating at the hands of the president on the budget resolution, and they were looking to even things up. Unexpectedly, they were handed a wonderful issue with which to scourge the administration. Speaker Thomas P. "Tip" O'Neill, called the proposal "despicable" and a "rotten thing to do." Representative Claude Pepper (D-Fla.) called the plan "cruel and insidious." House Democrats passed a resolution calling the proposals "an unconscionable breach of faith," while Senator Daniel Patrick Moynihan (D-N.Y.) introduced a resolution denouncing the administration's proposals. The Republican leadership managed to temper Moynihan's language, but still the Senate voted 96–0 for a resolution that put the Senate on record against any proposal that would "precipitously and unfairly penalize early retirees."[16] In the debate over the resolution, no Republican senators defended the administration's proposal.

The Democrats' partisan response to the administration's proposals was natural, given their beleaguered status at the time. They had suffered a number of setbacks, and the Republicans' proposed Social Security cuts allowed the Democrats to distinguish themselves from the Republicans in a beneficial manner and gain an advantage on an important issue. According to one Democrat: "When the White House announced that package, I couldn't believe it. It was the first crack in a solid wall of resistance. . . . If we hadn't jumped on the issue, we would have been declared politically non compos mentis." "It was like a bunch of duck hunters waiting in the bushes with the ducks too high to hit," a Republican remarked. "Along came this old turkey, and that was it." J. J. Pickle explained: "It was the only good thing that had happened all year [for the Democrats], and some couldn't resist the temptation to swing out. . . . That's as normal as breathing."[17]

Resisting the temptation to inflame the issue, Pickle sought to bring his subcommittee's bipartisan bill to the full Ways and Means Committee. But House Democrats opposed any further action on Social Security. The Pickle bill, after all, did call for some program reductions, and Democratic leaders were now on record opposing any cuts at all. Considering the Pickle bill would have spoiled the purity of Democratic opposition to cuts and possibly confused the public about who was on what side.

Democrats pressed the Social Security issue with enthusiasm. Representative Tony Coelho (D-Calif.) said: "The ball has been lofted to us. We've taken it and we're running with it. . . . We're not going to fumble it. It is without doubt our biggest issue, and there's no close second."[18] Elimination of the Social Security minimum benefit passed Congress as part of the massive reconciliation bill enacted in the summer of 1981. After burying the administration's proposal, the Democrats passed legislation restoring the minimum benefit under some circumstances.[19] This of course did nothing to resolve the funding problem but solidified the Democrats' reputation as defenders of Social Security. The Democratic party also made the Social Security issue the focus of a massive, extraordinarily successful direct mail campaign.

Faced with the Democratic onslaught, Republicans hunkered down and made no further proposals on Social Security. The White House was hurt badly by the issue; any further maneuvering short of agreeing to no program cuts would only have opened them up to renewed criticism. Discussions in the White House about trying once again to obtain some Social Security cuts were canceled, Stockman explained, because of the realization that "the Democratic campaign committee already had ten million letters ready to roll. They were preparing to unleash Claude Pepper again."[20] An aide to Robert Dole explained that the Democrats "wanted us to take the bait and announce our own package. They didn't want to do anything about Social Security but wanted us to give them more cannon fodder."[21]

Unwilling to serve as cannon fodder, the Republicans offered no new proposals. Republicans held a significant advantage over Democrats in the area of taxation. They were in the midst of reducing taxes, a very popular move, and they certainly did not want to tarnish their reputation on the tax issue by sponsoring a tax increase.

Stalemate developed because both Democrats and Republicans had symmetrical, offsetting advantages and disadvantages. Democrats had an advantage with respect to Social Security, and Republicans with respect to taxes. Both saw these issues as substantial political benefits that they were loathe to sacrifice. They also both recognized that they were unlikely to make significant inroads in the other party's advantage. Democrats could not credibly compete with Republicans in cutting taxes, and Republicans could not pretend to be stalwart defenders of Social Security. And so the Social Security trust fund inched toward bankruptcy as both parties protected their respective political advantages.

Comparing this stalemate with the Social Security bailout in 1977 affords some insight into the effects of divided party control. The 1977 experience, when the Democrats controlled both houses of Congress and the White House, suggests that unified party government is better suited to dealing with extremely contentious issues. In both instances, the Social Security system was faced with a tremendous financial challenge that could be dealt with only by means of politically unattractive revenue increases or benefit cuts. In 1977 the problem was dealt with quickly whereas in the 1980s it dragged on for two years. The important difference was that with Democrats controlling Congress and the presidency, there was little for either to gain in denouncing the other.

President Carter began the process by making a Social Security recommendation to Congress. It was ignored for the most part by the Ways and Means Committee, which wrote and passed its own legislation. But in doing so, it took no potshots at the president. The bill was potentially very controversial, especially because it called for large tax increases. Although President Carter did not like the bill that Congress handed him, he did not denounce it. There was no benefit for Democrats in attacking the package, regardless of how little they liked it, for delay in enacting the rescue would reflect badly on them as a party. Republicans could benefit from attacking the actions of the Democrats and distancing themselves from the bill, and they did. But as the minority party they were not well situated to stop the bill. Indeed, it would hardly have been politically helpful to stop the bill, for if they had, and Social Security ran out of money, Republicans would have had to bear much of the blame.

Budget Negotiations in 1987

As with Social Security, Democrats and Republicans in the 1980s manifested wholly incompatible preferences about how to solve the budget problem. Neither side had an entirely coherent plan for bringing the deficit to more reasonable levels, but Republicans were unified in their view that taxes should not be raised, and Democrats more or less so in their view that spending, especially on entitlements, should not be reduced. This was a perfect recipe for stalemate.

Gramm-Rudman-Hollings (GRH), the budget-balancing law enacted in 1985, had its automatic enforcement mechanism disallowed by the Supreme Court in 1986; nonetheless, its deficit targets remained in place. The Congressional Budget Office estimated that in order to reach the fiscal year 1988 deficit target of $108 billion, spending cuts and tax increases of $61 billion would have to be enacted.[22]

When President Reagan's fiscal year 1988 budget was unveiled in January 1987, it immediately became another of the several Reagan budgets pronounced "dead on arrival." It relied on optimistic economic forecasts, domestic spending cuts, and revenue-raising measures consisting primarily of asset sales and user fees. On paper, at least, it satisfied the GRH targets without cutting defense. But it found no friends on Capitol Hill. Numerous Democrats assailed it for its cuts in programs for the elderly, farmers, students, and others. Republicans offered only restrained defenses of Reagan's budget, since they were not pleased with the spending cuts it would require.

Achieving a significant measure of deficit reduction would require both domestic spending cuts and tax increases, for the simple reason that the president would not permit taxes alone to account for deficit reduction, the Democrats would not allow the domestic budget to absorb all deficit reduction and neither side could unilaterally impose a solution. Two questions remained, however. Would any deficit reduction occur? If so, how much of it would come from taxes and how much from spending? Throughout the spring and summer of 1987 there ensued a battle to determine answers to these questions.

Democrats were for the most part averse to cutting spending, but neither did they want to propose large tax increases. Walter Mondale, the Democratic presidential nominee in 1984, had advocated tax increases to cut the deficit and suffered a terrible defeat. After that, Democrats in Congress left it to Republicans to initiate tax increases. As long as taxes were "off the table," the only way to meet GRH was through large spending reductions, some substantial part of which had to come from domestic spending. President Reagan was similarly restrained, since his preferred solution to the deficit problem, large domestic spending reductions, had been repeatedly rejected by both parties in Congress. In 1984, a Democrat offered Reagan's budget as a floor amendment to the House budget resolution, and it lost by a vote of 1–401. Of course, if both tax increases and spending cuts were unachievable, then no deficit reduction would occur.

To unblock this stalemate, the new Speaker of the House, Jim Wright (D-Tex.), began a campaign to reintroduce the word "taxes" into political discourse. Even before his election as Speaker by the Democratic caucus in December 1986, Wright began speaking of the need for additional revenues. He mentioned the possibility of canceling a scheduled reduction in the income tax rate.[23] He proposed a tax on stock market transactions.[24] His enthusiastic support of taxes seemed to some Democrats to play into the hands of the president, and earned Wright the nickname "tax-of-the-month man."[25] Nonetheless, Wright apparently hoped that by daring to raise the tax issue, and surviving, he would bolster the courage of other Democrats. "They know I am willing to say the unsayable and lightning hasn't struck me," he explained. "I haven't been smitten like St. Paul."[26]

Wright's tax campaign provoked attacks from Republicans and only increased their dedication to resisting tax increases. President Reagan embarked on a series of speeches, denouncing Wright and the Democrats. According to a *Washington Post* writer, "White House officials [are] convinced that the best way for the president to capture the momentum he has lost in the Iran-contra affair is for him to lambaste the 'tax and spend' policies of the Democratic Party."[27] This tactic disturbed Ways and Means Chairman Dan Rostenkowski (D-Ill.), who normally had reasonably good relations with the White House. He complained that Reagan "hasn't been fair to us. I'm starting to interpret this president on the stump as not only somewhat irresponsible but enjoying it."[28] Republicans on the House Budget Committee completely refused to participate in drafting the resolution, apparently so that they would not be implicated in any of the revenue increases that it recommended or be compelled to offer an alternative. When the Ways and Means Committee later convened to write tax legislation, Republicans on the committee refused to consider any tax increases, even those previously supported by the president.[29] Their purpose, apparently, was to remain utterly pure on the tax issue so that they could denounce Democrats with complete abandon.

In late June Congress gave final approval to a budget resolution that went very much against President Reagan's wishes, proposing a tax increase of $20 billion and a spending cut of $7 billion. Although the president's budget had proposed more than $20 billion of revenue increases, nearly all came from non-tax sources, such as asset sales, and were far less offensive to Republican sensibilities than the Democratic proposals, which consisted of bona fide tax increases. To make tax increases less politically damaging to themselves, Democrats envisioned writing a tax law that put the burden on wealthy individuals. When the president vetoed the bill, Democrats would claim he was favoring the rich.

Congress applied still more pressure to the president to accept tax increases by reviving the Gramm-Rudman-Hollings budget-balancing law. This effort, spearheaded by Rostenkowski, gave GRH a new trigger to replace the one declared unconstitutional by the Supreme Court in 1986.[30] At the same time, the GRH "fix" relaxed the targets, raising the maximum allowable deficit from $108 billion to $144 billion. This reduced the amount by which the deficit had to be reduced from about $60 billion to a more modest $23 billion. It also threatened the president with defense cuts of about $12 billion if the sequester took place.

By the middle of October, it appeared that threats would not work. Congressional Democrats insisted that taxes be a substantial part of any deficit reduction legislation, and the president was equally adamant that taxes not be raised. Nor were the Democrats forthcoming with domestic spending reductions. Both sides seemed to prefer the onset of a sequester to compromise. Indeed, both sides seemed to regard the sequester as an excellent opportunity for bashing their opponent. President Reagan would claim that all the Democrats wanted to do was raise taxes, while the Democrats would blame the sequester on presidential inflexibility and intransigence.

Over time, the two sides moved farther apart rather than closer together. The president began by proposing a budget that called for some tax increases, but by October he swore to veto any tax increases. In June the Democrats proposed a budget consisting primarily of revenue increases but with a healthy dose of spending cuts as well; by October the House and Senate revenue committees had produced bills raising taxes by about $12 billion, but other committees had not produced legislation to yield the outlay savings promised earlier. Both sides moved from unbalanced but somewhat moderate positions to absurdly extreme ones. There was no compromise, and on October 20, the president issued the sequester order, initiating across-the-board spending reductions.[31] Both sides seemed able to find political advantages in the stalemate.

The Role of Commissions

These two brief histories illustrate the separation of powers and checks and balances at their most destructive. Madison argued in Federalist Paper 51 that "ambition must be made to counteract ambition," and in these cases we see that happening. Insofar as good government can be obtained by preventing government action, our constitutional system seems ideally framed. However, when the public weal requires expeditious government action, the competition engendered by separation of powers does not protect the public. The use of high-level, direct, interbranch negotiations ultimately helped to overcome partisanship and to allow the emergence and implementation of compromise agreements. These are just the sort of "cabals" and "intrigues" the Whiggish Founding Fathers feared and so strenuously sought to make impracticable through separation of powers and checks and balances.[32]

Negotiations conducted through the ordinary political process are both sequential and public—characteristics not conducive to success. Temptations to make partisan use of a statement or an offer from the other side can be irresistible. Moreover, neither party will want to initiate a reasonable offer through public channels if they believe that the other side will respond in a hostile manner.

Commissions or other forms of summit negotiations can be helpful in overcoming these problems by making it possible to offer proposals, and receive counterproposals, in private. The logic of bipartisan commissions is to have leaders of both parties, or their designated representatives, meet to negotiate a deal, excluding the press, public, and interest groups. Parties to the negotiation refrain from making inflammatory comments to the press and from revealing what has transpired during the deliberations. If and when a deal is agreed to, leaders from both sides announce and endorse it simultaneously. When deliberations are private, parties can make offers without risking denunciation by their opponent or by affected constituency groups. Because the public is excluded, there is less opportunity to use an offer from the other side to curry favor with constituents.

Once leaders have condemned each other and sworn never to compromise, it can be embarrassing to change positions. After it was badly burned on the issue of Social Security, the Reagan administration was reluctant to make another proposal.[33] Could the Democrats have gotten negotiations moving again by making a serious, balanced offer? Quite possibly; but after unequivocally opposing benefit cuts, it would have been difficult for the Democrats to make a public offer of benefit reductions. The commission relieved Democrats and Republicans of the painful necessity of making the next offer. They did not have to be the first to back down publicly from a previously announced position, nor did they risk being attacked by the other side.

Agreeing to summit talks, and adhering to their logic, is very significant, for it entails an implicit promise not to attack one's oppo-

nent. It means foregoing partisan attacks and implies a strong preference for reaching an agreement. Of course, entering into
negotiations does not guarantee they will succeed, or even that the
participants really want an agreement. If one of the parties prefers to
attack its opponent rather than reach an agreement, it can easily sab-
otage the negotiations by leaking to the press proposals from the
other side.

The National Commission on Social Security Reform

The National Commission on Social Security Reform was first suggested by the Reagan administration in September 1981, primarily
as a way of shedding responsibility for an issue that could only harm
the president. It was formally instituted by an executive order dated
December 16, 1981. Although it was eventually a great success, its
creation was not viewed auspiciously. Budget director David Stockman dismissed the commission: "Jim Baker had fobbed off Social
Security to a bipartisan study commission whose instructions were
to take a year to think about it."[34]

The commission was composed of fifteen members, five appointed by the president, five by the Senate majority leader, and five
by the Speaker of the House. The congressional appointments were
made in consultation with the minority leaders of each chamber. The
partisan balance of the commissioners was eight to seven in favor of
Republicans, although the ideological balance favored conservatives
over liberals by a margin of ten to five.[35] More important was the
inclusion on the commission of some of the most important and
influential members of Congress—among them Senate Finance
chairman Bob Dole (R-Kan.), Barber Conable (R-N.Y.), ranking
minority member of the House Ways and Means Committee, Bill
Archer (R-Tex.), ranking minority member of the House Social Security subcommittee, William Armstrong (R-Colo.), chairman of
the Social Security subcommittee of the Senate Finance Committee,
Claude Pepper, chairman of the House Rules Committee, Daniel P.

Moynihan, ranking minority member of the subcommittee on Social Security, and John Heinz (R-Pa.), chairman of the Senate Special Committee on Aging. In addition, there were two former members of Congress, Martha Keys and Joe Waggonner. Former Social Security commissioner Robert Ball and Lane Kirkland, president of the AFL-CIO and an important voice for American labor, also lent great prestige to the panel. Several members of the business community, appointed by President Reagan, completed the membership. The chairman was Alan Greenspan, a highly respected conservative economist with substantial government experience, who subsequently became chairman of the Federal Reserve System. The executive order directed the group to report by December 31, 1982—a deadline that was later extended to January 20, 1983.

It was highly beneficial to the purposes of the commission that its members were so likely to command respect for any recommendations they would produce; however, some of the members were extremists and unlikely to engage in the kind of compromise necessary to produce a substantial, bipartisan agreement. Pepper had built a nationwide reputation as a watchdog for the elderly, and it seemed unlikely that he would agree to substantial program cuts. Archer and Armstrong were vigorously opposed to tax increases. The commission's makeup virtually ruled out the possibility of a unanimous report, and without at least near unanimity the commission's conclusions would only engender more partisan bickering.

Early in the life of the commission, John Heinz suggested a fifty-fifty bargain—half increased taxes and half benefit cuts. This suggestion was rejected by the extremists on both sides. The commissioners met nine times over the course of the year and made no progress toward agreement. The commissioners were able to reach agreement on technical matters, especially the projected size of the Social Security deficit, and on the desirability of maintaining the fundamental structure and principles of the existing program. But they did not agree on the politically charged issue of how to eliminate the deficit.

The commission's staunch partisans were a problem, as were its open meetings with live C-SPAN coverage. With every relevant interest group either in the room or watching on television, it was impossible even to discuss concessions without raising a storm of protest. In December the group gave up on its quest for a solution.

Negotiations resumed in late December on an informal, secret basis among five of the more moderate commissioners—Moynihan, Ball, Conable, Dole, and Greenspan. They were joined by four representatives from the White House—Stockman, Ken Duberstein, Dick Darman, and Jim Baker, the White House chief of staff. This group consisted of sensible negotiators, none of whom was an ideologue. They were also adept at keeping their mouths shut and not leaking each day's developments to the press. Still more important, they had the tacit support of President Reagan and Speaker O'Neill in their quest for a compromise.

Robert Ball was the lead negotiator for the Democrats, speaking frequently with Tip O'Neill; Richard Darman and James Baker negotiated for the Republicans, clearing matters with the White House. They met throughout January and gradually crafted an agreement. The negotiations were conducted explicitly on the basis of a fifty-fifty division between cuts in benefits and increases in taxes. As one participant explained, "It became clear very early that, inasmuch as the Republicans wanted to solve the problem entirely with benefit cuts and the Democrats entirely with revenues, an even division would be required. What was scored as a tax increase had to be matched by a benefit cut."[36] All components in the agreement were classified either as benefit cuts, revenue increases, or as "unscored," a category reserved for changes that were not counted in either group. The major breakthrough was the decision to tax Social Security benefits of high-income beneficiaries. This provided a substantial savings that did not annoy either side excessively. The Democrats agreed to a permanent COLA delay and the Republicans to an acceleration of already scheduled tax increases.

After assembling a complete package and privately obtaining the backing of the president and the Speaker, negotiators took it to the full commission for approval on January 15, 1983. For the agreement to have any force, all interested parties had to agree to it, but none of them would commit before others had. Greenspan explained the situation: "The last thing was the tricky problem of getting everybody within an hour's time to all agree to this document, all contingent on everyone else's agreement. What we had going was that the President would agree if the Speaker would agree if the commission would agree."[37] And that is how it worked. The commission endorsed the plan by a surprisingly wide margin of 12–3; the dissenters—Waggonner, Archer, and Armstrong—did so in remarkably measured, moderate terms. The White House exerted substantial pressure on some of the president's appointees. Claude Pepper agreed—a surprise, given his previously unyielding opposition to benefit reductions. With the commission on record in favor of the plan, both the president and the Speaker endorsed it strongly and publicly.

The most contentious, partisan, and difficult issue in American politics became, almost overnight, an issue on which there was broad consensus. With the same plan drawing support from such unlikely sources as Ronald Reagan, Claude Pepper, and the leaders of both parties in the House and the Senate, the passage of implementing legislation took on an aura of near inevitability. The only important challenge in implementing the agreement was in finding additional savings to provide adequate financing in the long term. This was done by increasing the Normal Age of Retirement very gradually.[38] The legislation mirrored the commission recommendations on all important points and glided easily through both the House and the Senate. It received final approval from Congress on March 24, 1983, and was signed by the president on April 20.

There were a few dissenting voices. Federal workers opposed the agreement because it brought them into the Social Security system.

The American Association of Retired Persons fought the agreement because it cut benefits. Neither of these normally influential groups were effective in this case despite active lobbying against the deal. Many politicians would doubtless have been happy to placate senior citizens and federal workers by voting to strike these controversial provisions. But because they could not vote as these groups wanted without causing the entire package to collapse, members of Congress resisted pressure.

The commission succeeded because it avoided the necessity of negotiating a Social Security bailout in public. The commission format excluded the mass public and interest groups from the negotiating process. When the only audience for negotiations consisted of elites, one could no longer submit an unreasonable offer in hopes of currying favor with a constituency group. Similarly, there was no purpose to denouncing a proposal from the other side if interest groups could not hear ringing words uttered in their defense. Moreover, when virtually all politicians lent their support simultaneously, the risk of defection was minimal.

The Budget Summit of 1987

By October of 1987, President Reagan and the Democrat-controlled Congress had reached what seemed like an unresolvable stalemate on the budget. Sequestration under Gramm-Rudman evidently would have taken place if not for the intervention of a 500-point decline in the Dow Jones average on October 19. No one knew why this stock market crash occurred, and no one could tell if it was just a blip or the precursor of still larger declines. In any case, the Wall Street community declared that the federal budget deficit was too large and had to be reduced to return stability to the nation's financial markets.

The stock market did what Gramm-Rudman could not—it introduced a sense of panic and desperation that made deficit reduction so high a priority that it displaced considerations of partisan advancement. To calm the markets, President Reagan declared at a press conference that he would enter into negotiations with Congress in an effort to reduce the deficit. Everything but Social Security, he declared, would be on the table. Although Democratic leaders of Congress had frequently called for a summit meeting throughout the year, Reagan declined on the grounds that Democrats intended to use the discussions for the purpose of raising taxes. When he agreed to consider taxes, negotiations could proceed.

With the financial markets in continuing turmoil, and with Wall Street watching and waiting, the budget negotiators began their meetings under tremendous pressure to come to agreement. "A sense of apprehension, even fear, seems to have gripped negotiators on all sides of the table," Steven Roberts of the *New York Times* reported. "With the financial markets watching their every move, lawmakers say this is not the time to play their usual political games with the budget."[39] Senator Bennett Johnston (D-La.) explained that among the negotiators "the feeling is that the markets are really looking at what we're doing. We're very conscious of the markets." An unnamed Republican senator expressed hope that Wall Street would remain depressed because, he explained, "that's the only way we'll get together. We've got to keep the pressure on."[40] A Wall Street economist warned that a cut of only $23 billion, the minimum needed to avert sequestration, "certainly cannot help the markets."[41]

In order to to produce a deficit reduction of greater magnitude than the $23 billion sequester, the conferees continued meeting over a period of several weeks. The negotiations were not easy, for Democrats continued to protect their favorite programs while the Republicans tried to protect theirs. But the talks held promise because, for now at least, all sides were less interested than usual in scoring political points and more interested in reaching an agreement. The White House showed new flexibility on tax increases while Democrats showed greater flexibility on domestic spending. By November 10, one participant could say that "I think people see the outlines of a plan through the mist,"[42] and on November 20, an agreement on a

$30 billion deficit reduction was signed. Apparently the group had come close to agreement on a much larger reduction involving highly controversial limits on entitlement COLAs, "but the idea was dropped when neither Administration negotiators nor congressional leaders could figure out how to limit the political damage to their colleagues' satisfaction."[43]

The agreement was not as sweeping as many hoped but it was sufficient to forestall Gramm-Rudman. "We are sending the right message at the right time," Reagan claimed as he and congressional leaders announced the plan. The agreement, he said, was "a blueprint that sends a strong signal both at home and abroad that together we can and will get our deficit under control and keep it that way." Speaker Wright defended it as a reasonable compromise: "Nobody gets everything he wants. . . . It is a demonstration that in time of stress, the administrative and executive, as well as the legislative branches of government, can work together, even when they are in the hands of different political parties."[44] Although many of the participants in the negotiations worried that there would be great difficulty in persuading Congress to pass implementing legislation, in fact the legislation moved through Congress rather easily.

When and Why Summits Work
Summit negotiations work when both parties, especially their top leaders, want an agreement, and when the alternative is immediate disaster. These conditions prevailed in both cases discussed here, as well as in the 1990 budget summit, which also produced a bipartisan agreement. In the case of two failed summits, the National Economic Commission and the Pepper Commission, there was little desire on either side to compromise in order to reach an agreement, probably because no dire consequences were threatening.

The National Economic Commission (NEC), set up in late 1987 to reach a consensus on how to balance the budget, was based on the successful model of the Social Security Commission. Behind the

NEC lurked the hope that if reasonable people would only sit down in a nonpartisan atmosphere and think hard about the budget deficit, they would come up with a solution. Of course, the solution they would arrive at, being reasonable people, is some form of a "share-the-pain" formula of tax increases, defense cuts, and domestic spending cuts. Moderate politicians have been speaking for years of such a "grand compromise"; the NEC was envisioned as the means of implementing that compromise.

The foregoing logic would be quite compelling if politicians were primarily interested in reaching an agreement. Unfortunately, politicians' strategies for gaining and retaining political support doomed the NEC. George Bush ran for president with the slogan "read my lips—no new taxes." This promise certainly helped him defeat Bob Dole for the Republican nomination, and it probably also helped in the general election.[45] Throughout the campaign he found the NEC a useful target, labeling it a tax increase commission. The NEC finished its deliberations in 1989, President Bush's first year in office, when it was too early for him to consider breaking his most prominent campaign pledge. Nor was there room for compromise on the Democratic side. When Bob Strauss, a Democratic commissioner, discussed the possibility of Social Security cuts, he was bitterly criticized within his party and forced to retract the heresy. Ultimately, the commission majority issued a vacuous report that made virtually no substantive recommendations. The minority Democrats all dissented and the commission disbanded having made no contribution to solving the deficit problem.[46]

The United States Bipartisan Commission on Comprehensive Health Care, also known as the Pepper Commission, was established to find solutions to the problems of providing long-term care for the elderly and broadening access to health care for the uninsured. Like the NEC, its prestigious members were likely to generate legitimacy for an agreement should one emerge. It failed to generate a bipartisan consensus on health care because there was no pressure for an immediate resolution to the problem. Lacking pressure to solve the problem, neither Democrats nor Republicans were willing to engage in the kind of compromise necessary to reach an agreement.

As for long-term care for the elderly, the commission agreed by a bipartisan vote of 11–4 upon a government-financed plan for nursing home and in-home care. Nonetheless, this agreement was virtually meaningless because the commission did not address the crucial question of how the plan would be financed. Given the budgetary situation of 1990, an agreement on what to do, but not on how to pay for it, would not produce action. One commissioner, Pete Stark (D-Calif.), summed up the situation: "We didn't do our job. We didn't figure out how to pay for it. There is no tax fairy out there who is going to pull it out from under a pillow." As for the reason for the failure, Stark remarked that there was not "enough pressure to bring us together."[47]

Not even a fictional accord emerged on the issue of health care access. When it became apparent that a majority of the commission favored an ambitious proposal, the Bush White House apparently told Republican commissioners that they did not want a bipartisan recommendation to emerge. The White House wanted to avoid pressure for a new and costly program at a time of great pressure to reduce the deficit. Republican commissioners complied and the proposal passed on an eight to seven party line vote.

In order for a plan providing a comprehensive solution to either problem to be approved, taxes would have to be increased, and to this Republicans would not, or could not, agree. A less expensive alternative to comprehensive care would be a set of piecemeal reforms which, while they would not solve the whole problem, would presumably address some of the worst symptoms of the American health care system. Many Democrats cherish the idea of national health insurance and wanted to use the commission as a vehicle for advancing that cause. They were not interested in meliorative reform, because it might undermine support for comprehensive reform. A balanced proposal was the only kind that could pass, but given the political incentives of Democrats and Republicans, and the absence of a widely perceived health care crisis, neither side found a moderate proposal attractive.

Commissions and summit negotiations became a routine feature in American government in the 1980s, and we can expect they will continue to be useful in the future, especially under divided party government. Yet a puzzle surrounds their use to resolve partisan stalemate: deadlock has occurred with great frequency in American politics, but summits were virtually unknown prior to the 1980s. Why have they now come into use as a means of breaking deadlock?

Bipartisan summit negotiations are particularly helpful when action must be taken on highly distasteful legislation. Summit negotiations have become prominent because the number of issues on which decisions had to be made quickly has increased. Normally, in a democratic government few issues must be decided by a specific date. When agreement does not exist on an issue, decision can be deferred until one emerges. This has happened frequently in the presidencies of Eisenhower, Nixon, Ford, Reagan, and Bush. In the cases of successful negotiations discussed here, action was needed by a specific date, and both parties recognized this. I am unaware of any case in the last forty years, prior to the 1980s, in which these conditions pertained.

Summit negotiations are an excellent instance of "blame avoidance," the effort of politicians to shirk responsibility for controversial actions. Kent Weaver argues that blame avoidance strategies emerge when politicians must make choices that provide benefits to some constituencies but at a cost to others—in other words, zero-sum situations.[48]

Summits allow politicians to avoid blame for controversial decisions because the summit format obscures the origin of proposals. The summit, rather than any party or individual, can be blamed for unpopular policy choices; but a summit, unlike a person, cannot be held responsible.

The manner in which summits allow politicians to shirk responsibility makes them very controversial. It is widely believed that politicians in a democratic system must be accountable for their actions, for otherwise there is no democracy. This criticism is misdirected, however. Summits have no authority to implement agreements, only the capacity to negotiate them. Whatever they produce must later be voted on in Congress and signed into law by the president. Those who have supported a summit agreement must later defend their actions before their electorates.[49]

Summits succeed when the top political leadership in the executive and legislative branches are amenable to compromise. If political leaders are intent on indulging their instinct for partisan promotion, commissions will not help and summit negotiations will not occur. Commissions cannot impose solutions on leaders unwilling to hear or implement them. The role of commissions is to help overcome the uncertainty that attends public negotiations, and ease the emergence of an agreement that both sides see as advantageous. Because the temptations to seek benefit at the expense of one's rival are so great, politicians seem willing to forego the pleasures of partisanship only when the alternative is complete disaster.

6 · Advice for Moral Politicians

A half a loaf is
better than no bread.
—*Traditional saying*

Strategies of disagreement are the tactics politicians use
to avoid agreements that would move policy in a direction they ostensibly prefer, but which would either hinder their efforts to gain political advantage over opponents or reduce
the opportunity for getting a better deal in the future. These strategies have had a role in many important political debates and legislative episodes. In at least two of the most important domestic policy
issues of the post–World War II era—federal aid to education and
health care—strategic disagreement appears to have been responsible
for lengthy delays in enactment. It is an important element in political competition and is worthy of scholarly attention. There is also a
strong possibility that the politicians who employ it betray a fiduciary
trust to represent the interests of their constituents.

Politicians evidently consider strategic disagreement a sensible
tactic, and in some cases one can argue that it is better for the constituents, too, at least in the long run. This logic goes as follows: Passing
a compromise bill today will make it harder to pass a better bill in
the future. Therefore, constituents will be best served by passing no
bill today, because even though they will suffer in the short run, in
the long run the higher stream of benefits will more than compensate
for the period during which they must do without.

I will argue here, briefly and unscientifically, that politicians ought to make less use of strategies of disagreement and be more willing to take half a loaf. Politicians are commonly mistaken in believing that by holding out for the whole loaf they can do their constituents a favor. The benefits of holding out can easily be exaggerated and the costs ignored.

Strategies of disagreement may be optimal for the politicians who employ them, but they are not necessarily so for the people whose interests the politicians purport to represent. There is a potential conflict of interest between representatives and constituents, created by imperfect monitoring by constituents. When constituents pay little attention to politics and do not understand either policy or questions of feasibility, they are unable to evaluate a compromise to determine if it is the best that could be gotten under the circumstances, and thus worth adopting, or a sellout by their representative. When a single action or proposal is subjected to alternative interpretations by contending politicians, it becomes virtually impossible for the constituents to know what to think, and equally impossible for politicians who take controversial actions to make convincing explanations to their constituents. Nervous politicians are unlikely to enter into an agreement that they will be able to explain only with difficulty. Some potential gains for constituents will thus be unrealized, and this is a very real cost of poor monitoring by constituents.

Better monitoring by constituents would eliminate two sources of strategic disagreement—the problem of explaining compromise and the concern that accepting a compromise would diminish an advantage in the public mind. If constituents had the same understanding of politics and policy that representatives do, strategic disagreement would lose much of its value as a tactic. If constituents were well informed, parties and politicians would not worry that agreeing to a compromise would eliminate the distinction between parties and groups. Constituents would know that agreeing to a compromise in order to pass a bill may hide but does not eliminate the differences between contending parties and politicians. Well-informed constituents would be able to distinguish between a betrayal and a compromise that is the best that can be gotten under the circumstances. Well-informed constituents would know that support for an amendment that has no chance of passing is a symbolic action that means nothing. If constituents were more knowledgeable and attentive, obfuscatory tactics would fail, and politicians would not use them.

Even if constituents had complete information about their representatives, strategic disagreement could still conceivably benefit constituents by getting them a better deal later. I wish to contest this reasoning by showing that two assumptions of politicians who hold out for more later are questionable under most circumstances. Holding out for more can be beneficial to constituents if (1) accepting a compromise makes it harder to get it all later, and (2) an opportunity to get it all will come along in the near future. Actually, however, adopting a modest program can make it easier to get the whole thing later. And while the future may prove more auspicious than the present for enacting one's favored program, it may also be less so, and predicting the future is risky business.

Contrary to the arguments of some purists, the enactment of a minor program may actually encourage, not forestall, the enactment of a full-blown program later. The argument that modest changes will preclude larger ones later rests on the dubious assumption that the adoption of a new program will have no effect on preferences of legislators or constituents. The adoption of a limited health care plan may encourage people to want more and generate formidable pressure for expansion, especially when the inadequacies of the limited plan are experienced and felt. Commonly, the establishment of a new program is quickly followed by the creation of organized groups of beneficiaries and service providers who support the program and lobby for expansions. Wilbur Cohen became suspect in social insurance circles because he gave assistance to Representative Wilbur Mills and Senator Robert Kerr as they drafted a minimal health care bill for the aged in 1960, which, some activists thought, might undermine future efforts. But Cohen did not see it that way. Martha Derthick writes that he and other Social Security Administration professionals "had concluded from long experience that a categorical public assistance program would not long stand in the way of social insurance. It had not done so in regard to old age or disability insurance."[1] If programs that exist do more to generate support than programs that *might* exist, having a meager program in place can be the best way to get a good program established.

A limited program can lead to further expansion by undercutting ideological objections to its growth. Conservative arguments against aid to education prior to its adoption included the charge that federal money would lead to federal control over the curriculum. Having a modest school aid program in place could help to get a bigger one adopted later, if experience showed that federal financial help did not necessarily mean the loss of local control. After the adoption of a program, the character of the debate over it changes, for the question is no longer an ideological one of what the government should do, but a more practical one of how the government can best fulfill the obligations it has undertaken. Sundquist reports that after the enactment of federal aid to education legislation in 1965, "The question would be, henceforth, not whether the national government should give aid but how much it should give, for what purpose—and with how much federal control."[2]

Consider the wisdom of the Democratic strategy of disagreement in the Medicare fight of 1960. Democrats avoided Republican offers of a program funded by appropriations rather than a payroll tax, financed partly by state governments rather than entirely by the federal government. Strong supporters of the social insurance approach could have been concerned that if Medicare were established on the wrong foundation, it would be difficult or impossible to get it made into a social insurance program later. This is a legitimate concern if the establishment of a program is a nonincremental choice that constrains future development of the program. There is no reason to believe that incremental improvements were impossible or even unlikely, however. If a few years' experience with the program showed that funding through appropriations was inadequate, a new law could be passed levying a payroll tax to support the program. If some states did a poor job of running the program, new legislation could be passed mandating minimum standards. If the benefit levels proved inadequate, they could be changed. The Medicare program, like most others, consists of many features that are largely separable, each of which can be modified in response to inadequacies and public pressure. Opponents of establishing new government programs commonly describe a new, small program as the thin edge of the wedge or a camel's nose which, even though it starts out small, will invariably grow and grow. This is a reasonable cause of concern for opponents and a source of hope for proponents. Repeated incremental adjustments to correct for observed problems in existing law can bring about substantial change over time, and provide a powerful logic for issue advocates to accept a modest program at first.

Holding out for a better bill at a later date makes sense if a better bill can be enacted relatively soon. But waiting is a risky strategy, for not only can circumstances get better, they can also get worse. The future is unpredictable and the opportunity to pass the better bill may not come soon. Holding out makes most sense when one expects political conditions to become more favorable for the enactment of the perfect bill. Politicians might believe that public sentiment is shifting in their favor or might anticipate that upcoming elections will deliver them enough control over the government that they can pass their preferred bill. But public opinion may shift and elections can turn out differently than expected.

Opportunities to pass important bills can be rarer than they seem, as the Democrats should have learned about health care. In 1974 the Democrats dismissed a Nixon proposal on health care on the grounds that after 1975 they would have a "veto-proof" Congress and would be able to pass national health insurance. With the Republican political world collapsing in 1974, Democrats must have felt confident that the day would soon arrive when they would no longer need to compromise. They were wrong. They got a veto-proof Congress, but the economy sagged, budget deficits rose, and adoption of a major new program became unfeasible. The next good opportunity for adopting a comprehensive health care reform did not come along for twenty years, when the Clinton administration in 1994 made health care a top priority. Even then, no program was enacted. No one knows when the next opportunity to pass national health insurance will appear.

Democrats gambled in 1960 that Kennedy would win the White House and that they would be able to enact a social insurance version of Medicare. They won the gamble but could easily have lost, and then the delay in enacting Medicare could have stretched on for years. Even so, President Kennedy was unable to overcome conservative opposition in Congress. It was not until after the Democratic landslide of 1964, and the election of Lyndon Johnson, that the enactment of Medicare became possible. Considering that it took the assassination of President Kennedy and the Republican nomination of Barry Goldwater to produce Democratic majorities capable of passing Medicare, it should be clear that the Democratic gamble of 1960 could easily have gone awry.

Even when the election goes as hoped and the advantaged party wins the White House and gains seats in Congress, its ability to pass a bill may not increase, because after the election members of the disadvantaged party will feel less pressure to pass a bill. The Democrats avoided an agreement on aid to education in 1960, won in the fall elections, but were unable to make use of the victory to pass a bill. Prior to the election some Republicans felt vulnerable on the issue, and became more than usually compromising; they engaged in strategic agreement and Democrats responded with strategic disagreement. But the Republican inclination to help dissipated after the election and Democrats were unable to pass the bills themselves. In 1960, forty-four Republicans supported aid to education legislation, but in 1961 only six did.[3] Federal aid to education was not passed until 1965, by which time the Democrats had huge majorities in Congress and needed no Republican help. Insofar as their goal was to help constituents, Democrats should have tried to pass the best bill they could get and then work at improving it later. When Jimmy Carter was elected president in 1976, he had large congressional majorities, which perhaps should have led to a legislative surge similar to that of 1965–1966, but it did not occur.

Because of the unpredictability of the future, the advantaged party should regard overtures from the disadvantaged party as opportunities to pass welfare-enhancing legislation rather than threats to their superiority on an issue. Refusing to compromise can be better for constituents, but one must be extremely risk acceptant to prefer no bill to an inadequate one. There is danger that a better bill can be obtained only much later than one expects, forcing constituents to make do without even a modest level of benefits for the intervening period. It is possible that the bill passed after the delay will be no better than the one that could have been passed earlier. It is possible that a compromise bill passed earlier would have evolved into a better bill, thus giving constituents the benefits of a modest program in the meantime, and speeding the arrival of better programs.

For an object lesson of the perils of strategic disagreement, consider Senator Ted Kennedy. He has sought for more than two decades to enact national health insurance, and has nothing to show for his efforts. He conscientiously avoided the compromises offered by Nixon and Carter. But he could not enact national health insurance, nor was he able to ride the health care issue into the White House. Long ago he should have accepted half a loaf, which really is better than no bread.

**NOTES
INDEX**

Notes

Introduction

1. David Mayhew shows that the vast majority of important laws pass by large margins. See *Divided We Govern: Party Control, Lawmaking, and Investigations, 1946–1990* (New Haven: Yale University Press, 1991), 119–25.

2. The problem characterized here is similar to what George Tsebelis calls "nested games." See *Nested Games: Rational Choice in Comparative Politics* (Berkeley: University of California Press, 1990).

3. Samuel Kernell makes this point in "Facing an Opposition Congress," in Gary Cox and Samuel Kernell, eds., *The Politics of Divided Government* (Boulder, Colo.: Westview Press, 1991), 87–112.

4. James MacGregor Burns, *The Deadlock of Democracy: Four-Party Politics in America* (Englewood Cliffs, N.J.: Prentice-Hall, 1963). Most recently, attention has focused on the problem of divided party government and its role in producing stalemate. See James L. Sundquist, "Needed: A Political Theory for the New Era of Coalition Government in the United States," *Political Science Quarterly* 103 (Winter 1988–89): 613–35; Mayhew, *Divided We Govern*; Morris Fiorina, *Divided Government* (New York: Macmillan, 1992); Cox and Kernell, *The Politics of Divided Government*; and David Brady, "The Causes and Consequences of Divided Party Government: Toward a New Theory of American Politics?" *American Political Science Review* 87 (1993): 189–94. The best discussion of solutions to problems of ineffective or slow government is James L. Sundquist, *Constitutional Reform and Effective Government* (Washington, D.C.: Brookings Institution, 1992).

5. Mayhew, *Divided We Govern*, 119–35.

6. The filibuster, however, is much more a Republican than a Democratic obstructionist tool. See John B. Gilmour, "Senate Democrats Should Curb Use of the Filibuster," *Roll Call*, January, 24, 1994, 5.

7. For a discussion of the idea of "zone of agreement," see Howard Raiffa, *The Art and Science of Negotiation* (Cambridge: Harvard University Press, 1982), chaps. 3–4.

8. Quoted in James L. Sundquist, *Politics and Policy: The Eisenhower, Kennedy, and Johnson Years* (Washington, D.C.: Brookings Institution, 1968), 303.

9. See Nelson Polsby, *Political Innovation in America: The Politics of Policy Innovation* (New Haven: Yale University Press, 1984).

10. Roger Fisher and William Ury have introduced a useful term, BATNA, or Best Alternative to a Negotiated Agreement. The worse the BATNA for a participant in a negotiation, the more willing he or she will be to accept an imperfect deal. *Getting to Yes: Negotiating Agreement Without Giving In* (New York: Houghton Mifflin, 1981).

11. Time is extremely important in negotiations. A deadline can increase the incentive to settle. If the cost of delay is greater for one negotiator than for the other, the one most willing to delay has more bargaining power. See Raiffa, *The Art and Science of Negotiations*, 78–90.

12. Ibid. 8.

13. The events of 1960 are detailed in chap. 2.

14. See Daniel P. Moynihan, *The Politics of a Guaranteed Income: The Nixon Administration and the Family Assistance Plan* (New York: Random House, 1973).

Chapter 1. A Bill or an Issue?

1. Quoted in Taylor Branch, *Parting the Waters: America in the King Years, 1954–1963* (New York: Simon & Schuster, 1988), 221.

2. Mark A. Peterson, *Legislating Together: The White House and Capitol Hill from Eisenhower to Reagan* (Cambridge: Harvard University Press, 1990), 84–85.

3. Quoted in James L. Sundquist, *Politics and Policy: The Eisenhower, Kennedy, and Johnson Years* (Washington, D.C.: Brookings Institution, 1968), 408.

4. Quoted ibid., 408, from *Congressional Quarterly Weekly Report*, June 19, 1959, 830.

5. Quoted in Michael Foley, *The New Senate: Liberal Influence on a Conservative Institution, 1959–1972* (New Haven: Yale University Press, 1980), 22.

6. Evans and Novak, *Lyndon Johnson: The Exercise of Power* (New York: New American Library, 1966), 143.

7. D. B. Hardeman and Donald C. Bacon, *Rayburn: A Biography* (Austin: Texas Monthly Press, 1987), 392.

8. On the importance of mobilizing factions to presidential campaigns, see Nelson W. Polsby, *The Consequences of Party Reform* (New York: Oxford University Press, 1983). See also Herbert McClosky, Paul J. Hoffman, and Rosemary O'Hara, "Issue Conflict and Consensus Among Party Leaders and Followers," *American Political Science Review* 54 (1960): 406–27.

9. Harry McPherson, *A Political Education: A Journal of Life with Senators, Generals, Cabinet Members, and Presidents* (Boston: Atlantic-Little, Brown, 1972), 170–72.

10. Evans and Novak, *Lyndon Johnson*, 120–21.

11. Ibid., 127. Robert Dallek, *Lone Star Rising: Lyndon Johnson and His Times, 1908–1960* (New York: Oxford University Press, 1991), 517–21.

12. Dallek, *Lone Star Rising*, 526; Branch, *Parting the Waters*, 221.

13. Evans and Novak, *Lyndon Johnson*, 127–28.

14. Quoted in Branch, *Parting the Waters*, 221.

15. Lawrence J. Haas, *Running on Empty: Bush, Congress, and the Politics of a Bankrupt Government* (Homewood, Ill.: Business One Irwin, 1990), 85–86.

16. Quoted in Joe Martin, *My First Fifty Years in Politics* (New York: McGraw-Hill, 1960), 10. For other accounts of the leadership contest, see Henry Z. Scheele, *Charlie Halleck: A Political Biography* (New York: Exposition Press, 1966), 183–84; Robert L. Peabody, *Leadership in Congress: Stability, Succession, and Change* (Boston: Little-Brown, 1976), 288; and Charles O. Jones, *Party and Policy-Making* (New Brunswick, N.J.: Rutgers University Press, 1964), 33–38. Halleck was in turn bumped out of the job by Gerald Ford in 1965, partly because Republicans were interested in a leader who would provide more "constructive alternatives" rather than the strident opposition of Halleck, partly because many of Halleck's conservative supporters were swept away in the 1964 election, and partly because younger members of the GOP wanted more consultation, and a greater role in the party, than Halleck had been willing to concede.

17. Steve Neal, "Charles McNary: The Quiet Man," and Robert Merry, "Robert A. Taft: A Study in the Accumulation of Power," in Richard A. Baker and Roger H. Davidson, eds., *First Among Equals: Outstanding Senate Leaders of the Twentieth Century* (Washington, D.C.: Congressional Quarterly Press, 1991), 98–126, 163–98.

18. See Lawrence J. Haas, *Running on Empty*.

19. Richard Fenno, *Homestyle: House Members in Their Districts* (Boston: Little-Brown, 1978), 162ff; and John Kingdon, *Congressmen's Voting Decisions*, 2d ed. (New York: Harper & Row, 1981), 47–54. The best known counterexample is provided by Representative Clem Miller of California who, over a period of several years, sent to his constituents letters that explained what he was learning as a new congressman about the complex world of Congress. Astonishingly, he did not take cheap shots at Congress; he sought to teach and explain. Clem Miller, *Member of the House: Letters of a Congressman*, ed., with additional text by John W. Baker (New York: Scribner, 1962).

20. Anthony Downs, *An Economic Theory of Democracy* (New York: Harper, 1957), chaps. 11–12.

21. Public opinion polls frequently ask respondents whether they think spending on a variety of programs is too high, too low, or about right. People readily offer responses, even when they have virtually no knowledge of the current level of spending or whether more money could be used well. Responses are probably mostly an indication of valence, positive or negative, toward the issue or program.

22. Robert Salisbury, "An Exchange Theory of Interest Groups," *Midwest Journal of Political Science* 13 (February 1969): 1–32.

23. Ibid., 30.

24. Nelson W. Polsby and Aaron B. Wildavsky, *Presidential Elections: Contemporary Strategies of American Electoral Politics*, 7th ed. (New York: Free Press, 1988), 26.

James Q. Wilson writes about "amateurs," who are much the same as purists. See his *The Amateur Democrat: Club Politics in Three Cities* (Chicago: University of Chicago Press, 1962).

25. Quoted in Richard Cohen, *Washington at Work: Back Rooms and Clean Air* (New York: Macmillan, 1992), 104. Humphrey himself may have started as a purist but Lyndon Johnson persuaded him of the merits of compromise.

26. Peggy Noonan, *What I Saw at the Revolution: A Political Life in the Reagan Era* (New York: Random House, 1990), 109.

27. Raymond Bonner describes a contest within wildlife conservation groups over the ban on ivory trade as a means of slowing the slaughter of elephants in Africa. Professional conservationists, he contends, believed that a ban was not desirable, but groups felt compelled to endorse the ban because they feared they could not explain alternative policies to their followers, and would lose them. "Crying Wolf Over Elephants," *New York Times Magazine* (February 7, 1993), 30.

28. *Why We Lost the ERA* (Chicago: University of Chicago Press, 1986), 178. More generally, see chap. 13, "A Movement or a Sect?"

29. George Tsebelis, *Nested Games: Rational Choice in Comparative Politics* (Berkeley: University of California Press, 1990), 122–23.

30. Lawrence S. Rothenberg shows that the "activists," a small portion of a group's total membership, can exercise extraordinary influence over the group's leaders. See his "Agenda Setting at Common Cause," in Allan J. Cigler and Burdett A. Loomis, eds., *Interest Group Politics*, 3d ed. (Washington, D.C.: Congressional Quarterly Press, 1991), 131–49.

31. Daniel P. Moynihan, *The Politics of a Guaranteed Income: The Nixon Administration and the Family Assistance Plan* (New York: Vintage Books, 1973), 336.

32. John C. Esposito, *Vanishing Air: The Ralph Nader Study Group Report on Air* (New York: Grossman Publishers, 1970).

33. Cohen, *Washington at Work*.

34. Quoted ibid., 106.

35. Haas, *Running on Empty*, chap. 8.

36. Quoted in Harry Overstreet and Bonaro Overstreet, *The Strange Tactics of Extremism* (New York: Norton, 1964), 27.

37. Moynihan, *Politics of a Guaranteed Income*, 336.

38. It is beyond the scope of this argument to show that group affiliations do in fact influence mass attitudes toward candidates. For purposes here it is enough that candidates do actively seek the support of such groups, and seem to see them as a means of establishing their legitimacy as exponents of issues.

39. On the notch problem, see Julie Kosterlitz, "Little Can Match a Notch Baby's Cry," *National Journal*, April 23, 1988, 1081; Julie Kosterlitz, "Costly Cushion," *National Journal*, November 18, 1989, 2824; and Robert J. Myers, *Social Security*, 3d ed. (Homewood, Ill.: Irwin, 1985), 172–77.

40. This disparity could be fixed either by taking away the windfall or by increas-

ing the benefits of successor cohorts. Neither of these is politically feasible. Taking away benefits, even those not deserved, is a formidable task, and raising social security revenues is also to be avoided at all costs.

41. The National Committee to Preserve Social Security and Medicare was founded in late 1982. Its first fund-raising appeal promised to send a printout of an individual's Social Security records in exchange for a $10 contribution. This fund-raising tactic met with severe criticism, since the Social Security Administration provides such information free, and the committee agreed to halt that appeal. Letters from the committee rely on "half-truths, distortions, and misleading statements," according to a Republican congressional staff member (Julie Kosterlitz, "Mailouts to the Elderly Raise Alarms," *National Journal*, February 15, 1987, 379).

42. Kosterlitz, "Little Can Match a Notch Baby's Cry."

43. Kosterlitz, "Mailouts to Elderly Raise Alarms," 379. For some interesting examples of alarmist mail, see *Misleading and Deceptive Mailings to Social Security Beneficiaries*, Hearings before the House Committee on Ways and Means, 100 Cong., 1st sess. (Washington, D.C.: GPO, 1987).

44. This is a perfect instance of "concentrated benefits, distributed costs." See James Q. Wilson, *American Government*, 5th ed., (Lexington, Mass.: D.C. Heath, 1992), 435–36.

45. In an effort to defuse the problem, studies by the GAO and a special commission were authorized, and both reported back that the notch babies were not being mistreated and that nothing should be done. The National Commission on Social Security and Medicare rejected these studies, however, on the grounds that they were "flawed and biased" and because members of the commission "had already made up their minds the notch was not a problem" (Julie Rovner, "Expert Panel Advises No Action to Fix Social Security 'Notch,' " *CQ Weekly Report*, January 28, 1989, 179.)

46. Joseph White and Aaron Wildavsky, *The Deficit and the Public Interest: The Search for Responsible Budgeting in the 1980s* (Berkeley: University of California Press and Russell Sage Foundation, 1989), 363.

47. *CQ Almanac, 1983*, 261–64.

48. R. Douglas Arnold, *The Logic of Congressional Action* (New Haven: Yale University Press, 1990), 10–11.

49. Anthony Downs, *An Economic Theory of Democracy* (New York: Harper & Row, 1957).

50. See esp. chaps. 12–13.

51. Benjamin I. Page, *Choices and Echoes in Presidential Elections: Rational Man and Electoral Democracy* (Chicago: University of Chicago Press, 1978).

52. Thomas R. Palfrey, "Spatial Equilibrium with Entry," *Review of Economic Studies* 51 (January 1984): 139–56.

53. Henry E. Brady and Paul M. Sniderman, "Attitude Attribution: A Group Basis for Political Reasoning," *American Political Science Review* 79 (December 1985): 1061–78.

54. Julie Kosterlitz, *National Journal*, 1989, 1604.

55. An advocate argued that "the bare-bones plan is just a decoy, a way of delaying action on more fundamental reforms that threaten the insurance industry." Decoy or not, people with bare-bones insurance are better off than people with no insurance, at least in the short run. In the long run, not having bare-bones plans may speed the enactment of "fundamental reforms." Michael deCourcy Hinds, "Movement to Sell Basic Health Plan is Found Faltering," *New York Times*, November 10, 1991, 1.

56. Cohen, *Washington at Work*, 41–43.

57. Sundquist, *Politics and Policy*, 187.

58. Quoted in John P. Roche and Leonard W. Levy, eds., *The Congress* (New York: Harcourt Brace & World, 1964), 55. Morse himself liked to filibuster, but, he said, never for the purpose of preventing a vote, only to delay a vote to educate the public and the Senate.

59. James Brooke, "Marxist Revolt Grows Strong in the Shantytowns of Peru," *New York Times*, November 11, 1991, 1.

60. See Morris Fiorina, *Congress: Keystone of the Washington Establishment* (New Haven: Yale University Press, 1977); David Mayhew, *Congress: The Electoral Connection* (New Haven: Yale University Press, 1974); and Arnold, *The Logic of Congressional Action*.

61. Thomas Romer and Howard Rosenthal, "The Elusive Median Voter," *Journal of Public Economics* 12 (1979): 143–70; "Political Resource Allocation, Controlled Agendas, and the Status Quo," *Public Choice* 33 (1978): 27–43.

62. One can even argue that the best strategy for liberals is to sponsor and support legislation that moves the status quo away from their preferred policy, because that would allow them to pass new legislation implementing a more ambitious change than would otherwise be possible.

63. Not reaching an agreement in advance of the election still provides the advantage of keeping the issue alive, however.

64. For simplicity, throughout this section I will refer to the Republicans as the party trying to offset a Democratic advantage, even though the situation can be and sometimes is reversed.

Chapter 2. Strategies of Pursuit and Avoidance

1. See Robert Blake, *Disraeli* (New York: St. Martin's Press, 1967), 450–80; and Maurice Cowling, *1876: Disraeli, Gladstone, and Revolution* (Cambridge, England: Cambridge University Press, 1967).

2. Joseph Califano, Jr., *Governing America: An Insider's Report from the White House to the Cabinet* (New York: Simon and Schuster, 1981), 88–135.

3. Charles O. Jones, *Clean Air* (Pittsburgh: University of Pittsburgh Press, 1975).

4. Martha Derthick, *Policymaking for Social Security* (Washington, D.C.: Brookings Institution, 1979).

5. Califano, *Governing America*, 88–135.

6. Stephen John Stedman, *Peacemaking in Civil War: International Mediation in Zimbabwe, 1974–1980* (Boulder, Colo.: Lynne Reinner, 1991), 20. Stedman quotes a leader of the Algerian insurgency against France, who said in 1958: "France must understand that a negotiation can no longer be entered into today on what Ferhat Abbas demanded with moderation in 1943. Our people have not eaten grass and roots in order to obtain a new statute given as a concession" (quoted 19). As the investment of the group increases, and as their capabilities rise, their demands go up accordingly.

7. Richard Cohen, *Washington at Work: Back Rooms and Clean Air* (New York: Macmillan, 1992), 41.

8. Quoted ibid., 112.

9. For details of the reinsurance proposal, see James L. Sundquist, *Politics and Policy: The Eisenhower, Kennedy, and Johnson Years* (Washington, D.C.: Brookings Institution, 1968), 291–92.

10. James C. Hagerty, *The Diary of James C. Hagerty*, ed. Robert H. Ferrell (Bloomington: Indiana University Press, 1983), 90. On another occasion, Eisenhower said, "As far as I'm concerned, the American Medical Association is just plain stupid." William Knowland suggested waiting awhile before pressing on with the reinsurance bill, to give the administration time to work with the AMA. Secretary Hobby "broke in to say that there was not any way they could do business with the top hierarchy of the AMA. She said that there was only a little group of reactionary men in charge 'dead set against any change' " (94).

11. In the 1970 Senate race in Texas between George Bush and Lloyd Bentsen, many liberals lined up for Bush. John Kenneth Galbraith took the view that Bush and Bentsen were equally undesirable, and urged Texas Democrats to support the Republican candidate—Bush. "A Bentsen victory," he argued, "would tighten the hold of conservatives on the Texas Democratic Party, force the rest of us to contend with them nationally, and leave the state with the worst of all choices—a choice between two conservative parties. The defeat of Bentsen, by contrast, will show Texas conservatives that their only chance of winning is to become Republicans. That is how it should be and what the two-party system is about." Quoted in Gary Wills, "The Hostage," *New York Review of Books*, August 13, 1992, 24. Galbraith evidently preferred a smaller, purer Democratic party in the Senate. Having conservatives elected to the Senate as Democrats obscured the choice between Democrats and Republicans.

12. R. Douglas Arnold, *The Logic of Congressional Action* (New Haven: Yale University Press, 1990), 5.

13. Daniel Kahneman and Amos Tversky have made this point repeatedly in a number of articles. See, for example, "The Psychology of Preferences," *Scientific American* 246 (1982): 160–71; and "Prospect Theory: An Analysis of Decision Under Risk," *Econometrica* 47 (1979): 263–91.

14. Nelson W. Polsby, *Consequences of Party Reform* (New York: Oxford University Press, 1983), argues that a party nomination system centered on primary elections rewards candidates who are able to mobilize factions, not candidates who are able to forge coalitions.

15. See John Barry, *The Ambition and the Power* (New York: Viking, 1989).

16. This has not always been true. In the 1950s and 1960s the Republicans were a party of small budget deficits, and even though they disliked taxes, they hated deficits more. Consequently, Republicans had to be nervous about proposing tax cuts, for it was likely that Democrats would outbid them. This happened in 1975 when Gerald Ford proposed a $16 billion tax cut; Congress passed a $22.8 billion tax cut. See Barbara Kellerman, *The Political Presidency: From Kennedy through Reagan* (New York: Oxford University Press, 1984), chap. 9.

17. For a history of early efforts to establish medical care programs for the elderly, see Robert J. Myers, *Medicare* (Homewood, Ill.: Irwin, 1970), 3–50.

18. The following paragraphs rely on Sundquist, *Politics and Policy*, 296–308.

19. Ibid., 296–97; Myers, *Medicare*, 35–36.

20. Alice M. Hoffman and Howard S. Hoffman, eds., *The Cruikshank Chronicle* (Hamden, Conn.: Archon Books, 1989), 157–58.

21. Statement to the president by Robert P. Burroughs, October 16, 1959, Arthur Flemming File 1959–1961 (2), Box 15, Administration Series, Eisenhower Library.

22. Memorandum of conference with the president, October 23, 1959, staff notes, October 1959 (1), Box 25, DDE Diaries, Eisenhower Library.

23. Bess Furman, "Flemming Weighs Help for Aged Ill," *New York Times*, February 5, 1960, 13.

24. Arthur Flemming explained that one of Eisenhower's aunts had had serious medical problems and it did terrible things to the family finances. Eisenhower had no aversion to social insurance, having lived with free military medical for most of his life (Arthur S. Flemming interview, June 22, 1990).

25. Ann Whitman, Eisenhower's personal secretary, reported in her diary for March 22, 1960, that General Persons "says he has whittled the original proposal by Dr. Flemming down from compulsory participation to the present plan that was first approved by the President and Vice President and then, Friday after consultation with legislative leaders the President changed his position. . . . Dr. Flemming tells me that the Vice President reversed himself, too,—and further I understand would not talk to Dr. Flemming on the telephone." This account indicates two retrenchments (Box 11, ACW Diary, Eisenhower Library). According to a newspaper account, Republican congressional leaders were "vigorously critical of his proposals" (*New York Times*, March 22, 1960).

26. Eisenhower seems to have opposed compulsion for reasons of expedience, not ideology, commenting derisively that "doctors are psychopathic on anything in-

volving compulsion." Legislative Leaders Meeting, March 22, 1960, Eisenhower Library.

27. Saltonstall, Nixon, and Eisenhower, quoted in Legislative Leaders Meeting, April 5, 1960, Eisenhower Library.

28. *New York Times*, March 23, 1960. Quoted in Sundquist, *Politics and Policy*, 303.

29. Beth Furman, "Nixon is Pressing U.S. Medical Plan," *New York Times*, February 21, 1960, 48; Beth Furman, "Voluntary Plan for Aged Studied," *New York Times*, March 18, 1960, 9; "Nixon Reported Seeking G.O.P. Aid for Liberal Bills," *New York Times*, March 21, 1960, 1; John D. Morris, "White House Parley Fixes Principles for Aged Care," *New York Times*, April 6, 1960, 1.

30. "Javits Plans Bill on Aged," *New York Times*, February 22, 1960, 25. At the request of Everett Dirksen, Javits delayed introduction of his bill to give the administration a chance to clarify its position. John D. Morris, "Policies on Aged Fixed at Parley," *New York Times*, April 6, 1960, 35.

31. ACW Diary, May 2, 1960, Eisenhower Library.

32. The enrollment fee was expected to cover only 13 percent of total expenses. The rest was to be paid jointly by the states and the federal government. The plan was to be administered as an intergovernment program, with state participation being voluntary. States and the federal government would each contribute $600 million (Sundquist, *Politics and Policy*, 304).

33. Austin C. Wehrwein, "A.M.A. Denounces Eisenhower Plan for Care of Aged," *New York Times*, May 6, 1960, 1.

34. "White House Plan Attacked," *New York Times*, May 6, 1960, 32.

35. Ibid.

36. John D. Morris, "1.2 Billion a Year Sought for Aged," *New York Times*, May 5, 1960, 1.

37. Ibid.

38. Austin C. Wehrwein, "A.M.A. Denounces Eisenhower Plan for Care of Aged," *New York Times*, May 6, 1960, 1.

39. *Social Security Amendments of 1960*, Hearings before the Senate Committee on Finance, 86th Cong. 2d sess. (Washington, D.C.: GPO, 1960), 163.

40. John D. Morris, "Nixon to Support Eisenhower Plan for Care of Aged," *New York Times*, May 7, 1960, 1.

41. Perhaps Democratic liberals always supported doing more than they proposed, but were restrained by a fear of appearing extreme. When the Eisenhower administration moved decisively in a liberal direction, the Democrats were freed to back legislation closer to their own true preferences.

42. Farnsworth Fowle, "Forand Bill Fight Pushed by Labor," *New York Times*, May 10, 1960, 27.

43. "Symington Begins Tour of California," *New York Times*, May 30, 1960, 32.

44. John D. Morris, "Nixon to Support Eisenhower Plan for Care of Aged," *New York Times*, May 7, 1960, 1.

45. "President and Congress," *New York Times*, May 31, 1960, 28.

46. Joseph A. Loftus, "Democratic Bills in Peril; Kennedy's Hopes Fading," *New York Times*, August 24, 1960, 1.

47. "Wider Aged Care Pressed by Nixon," *New York Times*, September 22, 1960.

48. Tom Wicker, "Senate Rejects Kennedy's Plan on Care of Aged," *New York Times*, August 24, 1960, 1.

49. Recognizing these difficulties, President Kennedy's Medicare proposal offered fewer benefits than the Forand plan, eliminating surgical benefits (Theodore Marmor, *The Politics of Medicare* [London: Routledge & Kegan Paul, 1970], 42).

50. Marmor, *The Politics of Medicare*, 63.

51. Ibid., 66–67.

52. This political dynamic produced the somewhat peculiar distinction in Medicare between the two parts, HI (hospitalization insurance) and SMI (supplementary medical insurance). Roughly, HI corresponds to the Democratic proposals for hospitalization insurance funded out of payroll taxes, and SMI is the Republican proposal for voluntary insurance for a broader range of medical care funded out of general revenues and individual insurance payments. See Myers, *Medicare*.

53. Marmor, *The Politics of Medicare*, 68–71.

54. Quoted in *Congressional Quarterly Almanac, 1974* (Washington, D.C.: Congressional Quarterly Press, 1975), 387.

55. Ibid.

56. *Divided We Govern: Party Control, Lawmaking, and Investigations, 1946–1990* (New Haven: Yale University Press, 1991), 142–74.

57. John B. Gilmour, "Senate Democrats Should Curb Use of the Filibuster," *Roll Call*, January 24, 1994, 5.

58. The following discussion is based largely on Califano's fascinating account in *Governing America*, 96–135.

59. Jody Powell, *The Other Side of the Story* (New York: William Morrow, 1984), 190.

60. Califano, *Governing America*, 113–16.

61. Ibid., 116.

62. Ibid., 117.

63. Ibid., 119.

64. Ibid., 128–29.

65. Powell, *The Other Side of the Story*, 190.

66. An encounter between Senator Robert Taft and newly elected President Eisenhower presents an interesting contrast with the Kennedy-Carter conflict. In a 1953 meeting with legislative leaders, Eisenhower's budget team presented their revisions to the budget they inherited from Truman. They proposed cutting about $8 billion. Senator Robert Taft, Republican of Ohio, vigorously objected to the meager reduc-

tions. According to Eisenhower, "Senator Taft broke out in a violent objection to everything that had been done. . . . He predicted that the acceptance by the Congress of any such program would insure the decisive defeat of the Republican party in 1954. He said that not only could he not support the program, but that he would have to go on record as fighting and opposing it." Taft acted like a senator with presidential aspirations, careful to distinguish himself from the president and eager to make his objections public, just as Kennedy did with Carter. In fact, Eisenhower had beaten out Taft in a contest for the Republican nomination in 1952, which Taft had also unsuccessfully sought in 1944 and 1948. But Taft must have recognized by 1953 that his chances of winning the presidency, once bright, had passed, and that there was no particular point in provoking an open confrontation with the president. In the budget meeting, no one else rose to support his objections, and Taft cooled off considerably. "Before the meeting was over he had the appearance of being a jolly good fellow who had merely expressed himself emphatically" (Robert H. Ferrell, ed., *The Eisenhower Diaries* [New York: Norton, 1981], 235–36.) Taft did not go public with his objections, becoming instead a team player. He fell in line and became, as Eisenhower described him, the president's "ablest associate on the Hill, and indeed, one of the stalwarts of the administration" (ibid., 269). The partnership between Eisenhower and Taft lasted only briefly because Taft died in August 1953, leaving Eisenhower with the much less able William Knowland to lead the Republicans in the Senate.

67. Derthick, *Policymaking for Social Security*, 346.

68. Robert J. Myers, "Where Will the Pending Social Security Amendments Take the Program?" *CLU Journal*, September 1971; reprinted in *Social Security Amendments of 1971*, part 2, Hearings Before the Senate Finance Committee, 92d Cong., 1st & 2d sess. (Washington, D.C.: GPO, 1972), 884.

69. Richardson also indicates that the administration takes into account its expectation of how the Democrats will respond when framing its initial offer (*Older Americans Act Amendments of 1972*, Hearings Before the Subcommittee on Aging of the Senate Labor and Public Welfare Committee, 92d Cong., 2d sess. [Washington, D.C.: GPO, 1972], 235).

70. See *Reports of the 1971 Advisory Council on Social Security*, House Document 92-80, 92d Cong, 1st sess. (Washington D.C.: GPO, 1971), 64–66.

71. See Robert J. Myers's comments on this subject in *Social Security Amendments of 1971*, part 2, Hearings Before the Senate Finance Committee, 92d Cong., 1st & 2d sess. (Washington, D.C.: GPO, 1972), 862-863. See also Derthick's comments on Myer's views in *Policymaking for Social Security*, 354–55n.

72. Derthick, *Policymaking for Social Security*, 355n.

73. Ibid., 359.

74. Derthick tells of how in 1964 Mills gave a speech to a Kiwanas convention in Little Rock, explaining his opposition to Medicare on the grounds that it was hard to reconcile with the level earnings assumption. Derthick, *Policymaking for Social Security*, 358n.

75. Author's interview with Arthur Flemming, June 22, 1990.

76. See Edward R. Tufte, *Political Control of the Economy* (Princeton: Princeton University Press, 1977), 30.

77. Author's interview with Robert Ball, June 18, 1990. According to Ball, the Nixon administration would have been happy for him to leave, but not in protest.

Chapter 3. Strategic Encroachment

1. Fred Greenstein, *The Hidden-Hand Presidency: Eisenhower as Leader* (New York: Basic Books, 1982), 122–23.

2. "Excerpt of a Cabinet Discussion," January 16, 1959. Ann Whitman File, Cabinet Series, Box 12, Eisenhower Library.

3. David S. Cloud, "Politically Inflamed Issue Settled as Budget Amendment Fails," *Congressional Quarterly Weekly Report*, March 5, 1994, 527–29; David S. Cloud, "House Leadership, Freshman Key in Budget Amendment's Defeat," *Congressional Quarterly Weekly Report*, March 19, 1994, 657–58.

4. Jill Zuckman, "Rehiring Preference Advocated as Family Leave Substitute," *Congressional Quarterly Weekly Report*, May 18, 1991, 1291.

5. Legislative Leaders Meeting, Eisenhower Library.

6. This story is recounted in Robert Bendiner, *Obstacle Course on Capitol Hill* (New York: McGraw-Hill, 1964), 130–39.

7. See James L. Sundquist, *Politics and Policy: The Eisenhower, Kennedy, and Johnson Years* (Washington, D.C.: Brookings Institution, 1968), 155–220; and Frank J. Munger and Richard F. Fenno, Jr., *National Politics and Federal Aid to Education* (Syracuse, N.Y.: Syracuse University Press, 1962).

8. William H. Riker has written extensively about the Powell amendment, arguing that it killed school construction legislation. See *The Art of Political Manipulation* (New Haven: Yale University Press, 1986), chap. 11; and *Liberalism Against Populism: A Confrontation Between the Theory of Democracy and the Theory of Social Choice* (San Francisco: W.H. Freeman, 1982), 152–56.

9. According to Riker, the Republicans supported the amendment as a way of killing the bill, and the northern Democrats because they could not readily explain a prosegregation vote. When the bill came up for final passage, the Republicans voted against it because they were opposed to federal involvement in local schools, and the Southern Democrats because the Powell amendment would prevent their schools from benefiting. An essential element in this story is the assumption that the Southern Democrats would have voted for the bill had the Powell amendment not passed. As I argue below, however, the bill would have failed with or without the Powell amendment. Thus, the whole argument concerning strategic voting collapses.

10. Legislative Leaders Meeting, July 10, 1956, 3, Eisenhower Library.

11. Quoted in Stephen E. Ambrose, *Nixon: The Education of a Politician, 1913–1962* (New York: Simon and Schuster, 1987), 436–37. Terrell Bell, Reagan's secretary of education, reports a similar interest by Reagan in education in an election year. In

order to keep Walter Mondale from capitalizing on the education issue in the 1984 presidential election, Reagan extensively discussed the need for education reform and protected the education department from budget cuts. Immediately after the election, Bell reports, Reagan lost interest in education and the budget was cut. "How could the so-called sensitive area of education become such a low priority in such a short time?" asked Bell. "The only difference was that the election was over." See Terrell Bell, *The Thirteenth Man* (New York: Free Press, 1988), 158.

12. "Eisenhower Backs Compromise Program to Give the States 1.5 Billion for Schools," *New York Times*, May 24, 1957, 8.

13. "Eisenhower Host to Forty from House," *New York Times*, June 13, 1957, 22.

14. "School Cut Denied," *New York Times*, June 14, 1957, 34.

15. Quoted in Bess Furman, "President Backs School Aid Plan," *New York Times*, June 26, 1957, 22.

16. Benjamin Fine, "President Pushes School Help Bill," *New York Times*, July 4, 1957, 15.

17. Bess Furman, "House to Take Up School Aid Bill," *New York Times*, July 24, 1957, 22.

18. Bess Furman, "Eisenhower's Aid Asked on Schools," *New York Times*, July 23, 1957, 19.

19. Quoted in Robert Bendiner, *Obstacle Course on Capitol Hill* (New York: McGraw-Hill, 1964), 136.

20. *Congressional Record*, July 25, 1957, 12752.

21. Ibid., 12750.

22. Henry Z. Scheele, *Charlie Halleck: A Political Biography* (New York: Exposition Press, 1966), 178–79. Scheele notes that Democrats "were particularly upset when Charlie, free by legislative rules to do so, removed his pro-administration speech from the *Congressional Record*." Nonetheless, the next day in the House some Democrats read Halleck's statement back into the *Record*.

23. Charles Tiefer explains the motion: "To be precise, the motion is not to strike the enacting clause, but for the Committee of the Whole to rise and report to the House with the recommendation that the enacting clause be stricken. The House then decides whether to accept the recommendation. Since a bill without its enacting clause is a nullity, the adoption of such a motion amounts to killing the bill. By tradition the motion is considered a rough and ungentle form of execution, and its use to kill a bill is a high stakes gamble by bill opponents" (*Congressional Practice and Procedure* [New York: Greenwood Press, 1989], 398–99).

24. DDE Diary, Eisenhower Library.

25. John D. Morris, "Democrats Blame President For School Aid Bill Defeat," *New York Times*, July 27, 1957, 1.

26. "Transcript of the President's News Conference," *New York Times*, August 1, 1957, 10.

27. ACW Diary, July 25, 1957, Eisenhower Library.

28. Quoted in Charles Lloyd Garrettson, *Hubert H. Humphrey: The Politics of Joy* (New Brunswick, N.J.: Transaction Publishers, 1993), 281.

29. Allan H. Ryskind, *Hubert: An Unauthorized Biography of the Vice President* (New Rochelle, N.Y.: Arlington House, 1968), 200.

30. C. P. Trussell, "Eisenhower Aides Try to Block Bill Outlawing Reds," *New York Times*, August 14, 1954, 5.

31. Transcript of Legislative Leaders Meeting, Folder L-15 (3), Box 2, Legislative Meetings Series, White House Office, Office of the Secretary Records, 1952-1961, Eisenhower Library, Abilene, Kansas.

32. Ibid.

33. *Congressional Quarterly Almanac, 1954* (Washington, D.C.: Congressional Quarterly Press, 1955), 334-35.

34. Carl Solberg, *Hubert Humphrey: A Biography* (New York: Norton, 1984), 158.

35. Ryskind, *Hubert*, 201.

36. Quoted in Solberg, *Hubert Humphrey*, 159.

37. Richard Norton Smith, *Thomas E. Dewey and His Times* (New York: Simon and Schuster, 1982), 504.

38. Susan Hartmann, *Truman and the 80th Congress* (Columbia: University of Missouri Press, 1971).

39. Joe Martin, *My First Fifty Years in Politics* (New York: McGraw-Hill, 1960), 195.

40. Scheele, *Charlie Halleck*, 125.

41. Phyllis Schlafly, *A Choice Not an Echo* (Alton, Ill.: Pere Marquette Press, 1964), 49. Schlafly's argument was that the Republican party's only problem was its tendency to nominate overly moderate candidates who did not "run on the issues." If they ran on the issues, she reasoned, they could not lose.

42. Quoted in Hartmann, *Truman and the 80th Congress*, 186. A popular political button at the time read, "I'm just mild about Harry."

43. Clark M. Clifford, *Counsel to the President* (New York: Random House, 1991), 193. For a fascinating discussion of this strategy, see Samuel Kernell, "Facing an Opposition Congress: The President's Strategic Circumstance," in Gary Cox and Samuel Kernell, eds., *The Politics of Divided Government* (Boulder, Colo.: Westview Press, 1991), 98-101; and Gary A. Donaldson, "Who Wrote the Clifford Memo? The Origins of Campaign Strategy in the Truman Administration," *Presidential Studies Quarterly* 23 (Fall 1993): 747-54.

44. Quoted in Cabell Phillips, *The Truman Presidency* (New York: Macmillan, 1966), 226.

45. The request for civil rights legislation seems odd in this context, since the main obstacle was less the Republican party than obstreperous Southern Democrats. It could serve no useful purpose to call attention to splits within the Democratic party,

which were at least partly responsible for the do-nothing character of the Eightieth Congress. Housing was a particularly apt choice, however. Cabell Phillips reports: "Senator Taft had sponsored a housing bill that had passed the Senate during the regular session but had been bottled up by the conservative oligarchy on the House Rules Committee. What the President was asking in this instance was that the Republican Congress pass a bill bearing the name of its most distinguished Republican leader. A neat ploy, indeed!" Being a good party man, Taft worked to kill his own bill (Phillips, *The Truman Presidency*, 227).

46. Martin, *My First Fifty Years in Politics*, 188.

47. Herbert Brownell, *Advising Ike: The Memoirs of Herbert Brownell* (Lawrence: University Press of Kansas, 1993), 80–82.

48. Clifford, *Counsel to the President*, 223.

49. Irwin Ross, *The Loneliest Campaign: The Truman Victory of 1948* (New York: New American Library, 1966), 136–37. See also James T. Patterson, *Mr. Republican: A Biography of Robert A. Taft* (Boston: Houghton Mifflin, 1972), 420; and Smith, *Thomas A. Dewey*, 512–13.

50. Herbert Brownell suggests another explanation for Republican intransigence. "Some Republicans," Brownell writes, "attributed the reluctance of Taft and the other Republicans in Congress to act . . . to their willingness to write Dewey off as a candidate. Dewey was not the kind of Republican they wanted to have at the head of the party when it regained the White House. If Dewey became president and ran for a second term, it would not be until 1956—and too late—that Taft and Vandenberg, who continued to harbor presidential ambitions, could run again." Brownell himself doubts that Taft was so motivated. See Brownell, *Advising Ike*, 81.

51. Clark Clifford says that in the midst of the campaign, Mrs. Truman asked him, "Do you think that Harry really believes he is going to win? He certainly acts that way." *Counsel to the President*, 189.

Chapter 4. Provoking a Veto

1. On the veto generally, see the discussion in Richard M. Pious, *The American Presidency* (New York: Basic Books, 1979), 203–10; Robert J. Spitzer, *The Presidential Veto: Touchstone of the American Presidency* (Albany: State University of New York Press, 1988); Richard A. Watson, *Presidential Vetoes and Public Policy* (Lawrence: University Press of Kansas, 1993); John T. Woolley, "Institutions, the Election Cycle, and the Presidential Veto," *American Journal of Political Science* 35 (May 1991): 279–304; and David W. Rohde and Dennis M. Simon, "Presidential Vetoes and Congressional Response: a Study of Institutional Conflict," *American Journal of Political Science* 29 (August 1985), 397–427.

2. Others disagree that the president's veto confers great power. As Daniel Ingberman and Dennis Yao explain, agenda control theorists "conclude that the president's veto translates into limited influence because the veto cannot increase the president's payoffs in conflict situations over the level obtained from the no bill (or

reversion) outcome. The reason is that the formal structure of the president-Congress interaction leaves the president with a take-it-or-leave-it choice between the bill offered by Congress and no bill at all" ("Presidential Commitment and the Veto," *American Journal of Political Science* 35 [May 1991]: 357–89). For the agenda control interpretation, see D. Roderick Kiewiet and Mathew D. McCubbins, "Presidential Influence on Congressional Appropriations Decisions," *American Journal of Political Science* 32 (August 1988): 713–36. For a criticism, see Steven A. Matthews, "Veto Threats: Rhetoric in a Bargaining Game," *Quarterly Journal of Economics* 104 (May 1989): 347–69.

3. Forcing the president to veto a popular bill is a kind of "blame-generating" strategy, parallel to the strategies of blame avoidance discussed by R. Kent Weaver in "The Politics of Blame Avoidance," *Journal of Public Policy* 6 (1986): 371–98; and *Automatic Government: The Politics of Indexation* (Washington, D.C.: Brookings Institution, 1988).

4. "Family Leave Veto Upheld," *Congressional Quarterly Weekly Report*, July 28, 1990, 2405.

5. Bills were passed and vetoed in 1985, 1988, and 1990. None of the override attempts were successful. After the 1985 bill was vetoed, Congress delayed the override vote until just before the 1986 elections. See Andy Plattner, "Democrats See Political Gold in Trade Issue," *Congressional Quarterly Weekly Report*, September 21, 1985, 1856; Elizabeth Wehr, "Textile-Quota Bill Clears Congress, Awaits Veto," *Congressional Quarterly Weekly Report*, September 24, 1988, 2666; and "Textile Quota Bill Falls to Veto Again," *Congressional Quarterly Almanac, 1990* (Washington, D.C.: Congressional Quarterly Press, 1991), 219.

6. David Mayhew, *Divided We Govern* (New Haven: Yale University Press, 1991).

7. Here and elsewhere I assume that the Democrats control Congress and Republicans have the White House only because that has been much more common than the present, reverse situation.

8. Julie Rovner, "Democrats Fail to Make Good on Freedom of Choice Act," *Congressional Quarterly Weekly Report*, August 8, 1992, 2360–61.

9. Dennis Simon shows that the probability of vetoes rises closer to the election. "The President Versus Congress: The House and Senate Response to Presidential Vetoes, 1945–1992." Presented at the 1994 Western Political Science Association Meeting, Albuquerque, New Mexico, March 10–12.

10. *Congressional Quarterly Almanac, 1959* (Washington, D.C.: Congressional Quarterly Press, 1960), 249–56; and Sundquist, *Politics and Policy*, 198–99.

11. Lawrence J. Haas, *Running on Empty: Bush, Congress, and the Politics of a Bankrupt Government* (Homewood, Ill.: Business One Irwin, 1990), 267–68.

12. Beth Donovan, "Smooth Sailing Isn't in Forecast for Election Law Revisions," *Congressional Quarterly Weekly Report*, November 21, 1992, 3666–67.

13. Samuel Kernell discusses the strategy of the presidential veto in "Facing an Opposition Congress," in Gary Cox and Samuel Kernell, eds., *The Politics of Divided Government* (Boulder, Colo.: Westview Press, 1991), 87–112.

14. On Ford's veto strategy, see A. James Reichley, *Conservatives in an Age of Change* (Washington, D.C.: Brookings Institution, 1981), chap. 15. On Bush and vetoes, see Charles Tiefer, *The Semi-Sovereign Presidency* (Boulder, Colo.: Westview Press, 1994).

15. Legislative Leaders Meeting, June 2, 1960, 3, Eisenhower Library.

16. Susan Hartmann, *Truman and the 80th Congress* (Columbia: University of Missouri Press, 1971), 87.

17. Richard Cohen, *Washington at Work: Back Rooms and Clean Air* (New York: Macmillan, 1992), 168–69.

Chapter 5. Stalemates and Summit Negotiations

1. Paul Quirk, "The Cooperative Resolution of Policy Conflict," *American Political Science Review* 83 (1989): 905–21.

2. John Petrocik develops at length the notion of "issue ownership" in "Divided Government: Is It all in the Campaigns?" in Gary Cox and Samuel Kernell, eds., *The Politics of Divided Government* (Boulder, Colo.: Westview Press, 1991), 13–38.

3. Roger Fisher and William Ury, *Getting to Yes: Negotiating Agreement Without Giving In* (New York: Houghton Mifflin, 1981).

4. Ibid., 79.

5. Andre Modigliani and Franco Modigliani provide evidence of the aversion of the public to making a sacrifice to attain a prospective good. They show that in 1981, survey respondents were not in favor of a tax cut that would increase the deficit, but that subsequently, once a tax cut did increase the deficit, they were not in favor of a tax increase to reduce the deficit! ("The Growth of the Federal Deficit and the Role of Public Attitudes," *Public Opinion Quarterly* 51 [1987]: 459–80).

6. Bargaining theorists discuss the utility of committing oneself to a particular course of action in order to increase bargaining power. See Thomas Schelling, *The Strategy of Conflict* (Cambridge: Harvard University Press, 1960), and *Arms and Influence* (New Haven: Yale University Press, 1966); and V. P. Crawford, "A Theory of Disagreement in Bargaining," in *The Economics of Bargaining*, Ken Binmore and Partha Dasgupta, eds. (Oxford: Basil Blackwell, 1987), 121–54. Daniel Ingberman and Dennis Yao argue that the president can increase his power by committing himself very publicly to vetoing legislation that does not satisfy specified requirements. "Presidential Commitment and the Veto," *American Journal of Political Science* 35 (May 1991): 357–89.

7. John Nash, "The Bargaining Problem," *Econometrica* 18 (1950): 155.

8. Howard Raiffa, *The Art and Science of Negotiation* (Cambridge: Harvard University Press, 1982), 52.

9. Schelling, *The Strategy of Conflict*. See also Schelling's essay "The Intimate Contest for Self-Command," in *Choice and Consequence* (Cambridge: Harvard University Press, 1984).

10. R. Douglas Arnold contends that the actions of members of Congress are

guided by their estimates of the "potential preferences" of constituents—"preferences which legislators believe might easily be created either by interested parties dissatisfied with legislators' decisions or by future challengers searching for good campaign issues." Legislators are reluctant to take positions or cast votes that will provide rivals with good ammunition. See *The Logic of Congressional Action* (New Haven: Yale University Press, 1990), 10–11.

11. The discussion here is limited to relatively symmetrical cases in which neither side can impose a unilateral solution and a compromise is therefore necessary.

12. The use of general revenues had been advocated for many years by some Social Security experts, but it was somewhat impractical in an era of $100 billion annual deficits. According to Senator William Armstrong (R-Colo.), the idea of using general revenues to assist Social Security was "like asking Amtrak to bail out Conrail." Spencer Rich, "Plight of Social Security is Being Exaggerated, Democrats Charge," *Washington Post*, July 8, 1981, 1.

13. On the Pickle bill, see Timothy B. Clark, "Saving Social Security—Reagan and Congress Face Some Unpleasant Choices," *National Journal*, June 13, 1981.

14. David Stockman, *The Triumph of Politics: Why the Reagan Revolution Failed* (New York: Harper and Row, 1986), 184.

15. Ibid., 190–91; Robert J. Myers, *Social Security*, 3d ed. (Homewood, Ill.: Irwin, 1985), 283.

16. Helen Dewar, "Senate Unanimously Rebuffs President on Social Security," *Washington Post*, May 21, 1981.

17. Paul Light, *Artful Work* (New York: Random House, 1985), 125–28.

18. Ibid., 129.

19. The reconciliation bill contained other significant benefit reductions that were not later restored. These included (1) the elimination of child student benefits with respect to retired, deceased, or disabled workers; (2) restrictions on lump-sum death benefits; and (3) the introduction of a cap on disability benefits where other disability benefits are payable.

20. Stockman, *The Triumph of Politics*, 310.

21. Ibid.

22. Tom Kenworthy, "Democrats Ask Reagan to Be 'Realistic' on Budget," *Washington Post*, February 18, 1987.

23. David S. Broder, "Block Tax Cuts for Rich, Wright Says," *Washington Post*, January 10, 1987.

24. Tom Kenworthy, "Wright Suggests Taxing Stock Transactions," *Washington Post*, March 4, 1987.

25. David S. Broder, "Democrats Find Taxes Treacherous Territory," *Washington Post*, March 15, 1987.

26. Tom Kenworthy, "Wright Launches Push For Tax Rise Support," *Washington Post*, March 5, 1987.

27. Tom Kenworthy, "$1 Trillion Hill Budget Blueprint Nears Final Passage in the Senate," *Washington Post*, June 25, 1987.

28. Tom Kenworthy, "Democrats Plan New Tactics on Fiscal Front," *Washington Post*, July 6, 1987.

29. Anne Swardson, "Tax Bill Drafting Session Halts After GOP Balks," *Washington Post*, October 2, 1987.

30. See Joseph White and Aaron Wildavsky, *The Deficit and the Public Interest: The Search for Responsible Budgeting in the 1980s* (Berkeley: University of California Press, 1989), chaps. 19 and 21; and John B. Gilmour, *Reconcilable Differences? Congress, the Budget Process, and the Deficit* (Berkeley: University of California Press, 1990), chap. 5.

31. Judith Havemann, "President Activates Budget-Cut Mechanism," *Washington Post*, November 21, 1987.

32. Richard Hofstadter, *The Idea of a Party System* (Berkeley: University of California Press, 1969).

33. Light, *Artful Work*, 175.

34. Stockman, *The Triumph of Politics*, 332.

35. Light, *Artful Work*, 191.

36. Robert Ball interview with author, June 18, 1990.

37. Light, *Artful Work*, 191.

38. The original retirement age of sixty-five would be maintained until the year 2002, after which it would rise gradually to sixty-seven in 2027.

39. Steven Roberts, "Parley on Budget Opened," *New York Times*, October 29, 1987.

40. Ibid.

41. Robert A. Bennett, "Wall St. Sees Market Drop in a Small Budget Cut," *New York Times*, November 19, 1987.

42. Jonathan Feuerbringer, "Accord Held Near on Deficit Figures," *New York Times,* November 11, 1987.

43. Jonathan Feuerbringer, "Agreement Signed to Reduce Deficit $30 billion in 1988," *New York Times,* November 21, 1987.

44. Tom Kenworthy, "Reagan, Hill Agree To Cut $76 Billion," *Washington Post*, November 21, 1987.

45. Breaking the pledge probably helped him lose the 1992 election, however. This is as good an example as exists that the things that help get one elected can make governing impossible after the election, and the things a politician must do in order to govern make reelection impossible.

46. David Rapp, "Deficit Panel to Close Up Shop," *Congressional Quarterly Weekly Report*, February 25, 1989, 374.

47. Julie Rovner, "Pepper Commission Splinters Over Health Financing," *Congressional Quarterly Weekly Report*, March 3, 1990, 667–68.

48. R. Kent Weaver, "The Politics of Blame Avoidance," *Journal of Public Policy* 6

(1986): 371–98; and *Automatic Government: The Politics of Indexation* (Washington, D.C.: Brookings Institution, 1988).

49. For an alternative view, emphasizing the "vital role deliberation plays in enlightening public opinion and forging a national consensus to support government action," see Gerald B. H. Solomon and Donald Wolfensberger, "The Decine of Deliberative Democracy in the House and Proposals for Reform," *Harvard Journal on Legislation* 31 (1994): 353.

Chapter 6. Advice for Moral Politicians

1. Martha Derthick, *Policymaking for Social Security* (Washington, D.C.: Brookings Institution, 1979), 323–24.

2. James L. Sundquist, *Politics and Policy: The Eisenhower, Johnson, and Kennedy Years* (Washington, D.C.: Brookings Institution, 1968), 216.

3. Ibid., 193.

Index